The TEACHER *as* ASSESSMENT LEADER

Edited by **Thomas R. Guskey**

CASSANDRA ERKENS
WILLIAM M. FERRITER
MICHELLE GOODWIN
TAMMY HEFLEBOWER
TOM HIERCK
CHRIS JAKICIC
SHARON V. KRAMER
JEFFRY OVERLIE
AINSLEY B. ROSE
NICOLE M. VAGLE
ADAM YOUNG

Solution Tree | Press

a division of
Solution Tree

555 North Morton Street
Bloomington, IN 47404
800.733.6786 (toll free) / 812.336.7700
FAX: 812.336.7790
email: info@solution-tree.com
solution-tree.com

Visit **go.solution-tree.com/assessment** to download materials associated with this book.

Printed in the United States of America

13 12 11 10 09   2 3 4 5

FSC
Mixed Sources
Product group from well-managed
forests and other controlled sources
Cert no. SW-COC-002283
www.fsc.org
© 1996 Forest Stewardship Council

Library of Congress Cataloging-in-Publication Data

The teacher as assessment leader / edited by Thomas R. Guskey ... [et al.].
    p. cm.
  Includes bibliographical references and index.
  ISBN 978-1-934009-49-9 (perfect bound) -- ISBN 978-1-935249-11-5 (library binding) 1. Educational tests and measurements. 2. Academic achievement--Testing. 3. Teachers. I. Guskey, Thomas R.
  LB3051.T32 2009
  371.26--dc22
                            2009020480

_____

Solution Tree
Jeffrey C. Jones, CEO and President

Solution Tree Press
President: Douglas M. Rife
Publisher: Robert D. Clouse
Director of Production: Gretchen Knapp
Managing Production Editor: Caroline Wise
Proofreader: Elisabeth Abrams
Cover Designer: Amy Shock
Text Designer: Raven Bongiani
Compositor: Amy Shock

Table of Contents

Chapter 11
Differentiated Pathways to Success

THOMAS R. GUSKEY

 Thomas R. Guskey, PhD, is professor of educational psychology in the College of Education at the University of Kentucky. A graduate of the University of Chicago, he served as director of research and development for Chicago Public Schools and was the first director of the Center for the Improvement of Teaching and Learning, a national research center.

Dr. Guskey coedited the *Experts in Assessment* series and was a contributor to the assessment anthology *Ahead of the Curve: The Power of Assessment to Transform Teaching and Learning.* He has been featured on the National Public Radio programs *Talk of the Nation* and *Morning Edition.*

Dr. Guskey is listed in the National Staff Development Council's *Leaders in Staff Development.* He is the only person to have won the Council's Book of the Year Award twice and the Article of the Year Award three times. His work has been honored by numerous organizations, and his articles have appeared in prominent research journals, as well as *Educational Leadership, Phi Delta Kappan,* and *The School Administrator.* He served on the policy research team of the National Commission on Teaching and America's Future, the task force to develop the *National Standards for Staff Development,* and was recently named a Fellow in the American Educational Research Association, which also honored him in 2006 for his outstanding contribution relating research to practice.

Introduction

Thomas R. Guskey

Teachers at all levels of education today are beginning to recognize the value of classroom formative assessments. They are coming to see how the results from well designed assessments *for* learning (Stiggins, 2008) can be used both to enhance the quality of their teaching and to guide improvements in student learning. Instead of treating assessments as only evaluation devices that mark the end of an instructional unit, more and more teachers today realize that formative assessments offer exactly what they have always wanted: a practical and efficient means to make their teaching better and to help all of their students learn better.

Ironically, most teachers believe that using classroom assessments to guide improvements in teaching and learning is a relatively new idea in education. But in truth, the value of "formative" assessments was identified nearly four decades ago by true giants in the field of education. In their 1971 book *Handbook on Formative and Summative Evaluation of Student Learning*, Benjamin Bloom, Thomas Hastings, and George Madaus described the benefits of offering students regular feedback on their learning progress through classroom formative assessments. Bloom went on to outline specific strategies teachers could use to implement formative assessments as part of regular classroom routines, both to improve student learning and to reduce gaps in the achievement of different subgroups of students (Bloom, 1971). It was Bloom who initiated the phrase "formative assessments" and who provided practical guidance for their use in modern classrooms (Guskey, 2006, 2007).

Although it has taken quite a while for the idea to catch on, formative classroom assessments are now used in kindergarten through college and university classes. Many teachers learned about formative assessments through the work of Paul Black and Dylan Wiliam (1998), who verified what Bloom and his colleagues told us decades ago: regular formative assessments paired with well-planned corrective activities offer one of the most powerful tools teachers can use to help all students learn well (Bloom, Madaus, & Hastings, 1981; Guskey, 2008).

This book is designed to offer teacher leaders practical ideas on how to make the best and most effective use of classroom formative assessments. Unlike other books for teachers whose authors base their ideas on opinions or conjectures about what they think should be done, however, the authors of each of these chapters derived their ideas through hard-earned experience. Their perspectives have been shaped by the successes and failures they have known in real school and classroom settings. They are not writing from an ivory tower or from the comfort of a research center, but from the front lines, where they have learned firsthand about the real challenges and difficulties that teachers face in their efforts to improve the learning outcomes of all students.

Part One of this volume focuses on "Laying the Foundation of Assessment Literacy." We begin with Cassandra Erkens' chapter on "Developing Our Assessment Literacy." Cassandra describes the importance of collaboration in efforts designed to enhance teachers' assessment literacy. After identifying several fallacies that impede the development of a more formative orientation toward assessment, she explains how working in communities and learning by doing can help teachers at all levels improve the quality of the assessment instruments they develop and use.

In the next chapter on "Assessment That Makes Sense," Chris Jakicic offers her ideas about the crucial differences between formative and summative assessments. She then goes on to describe in detail the elements of a balanced assessment system that utilizes the best properties of formative assessments *for* learning as well as summative assessments *of* learning.

William Ferriter's chapter "Yes, I Can: Responsible Assessment in an Era of Accountability" describes a five-step process for helping learning teams develop assessments that accurately and effectively measure what we expect students to learn. After outlining the five steps, William offers lots of practical examples on how this can be accomplished.

Part Two on "Collecting, Interpreting, and Reporting Data," begins with Michelle Goodwin's chapter, "Matchmaker, Matchmaker, Write Me a Test." Michelle first presents a four-step model for ensuring the proper alignment of learning targets with assessment types. After discussing the implications of this process, she shares down-to-earth advice on how to adapt assessment formats to specific learning goals in a wide variety of subject areas.

Tammy Heflebower's chapter on "Proficiency: More Than a Grade" stresses the importance of relevant, timely, and trustworthy information about student performance in successful improvement efforts. She then explains how teachers can understand and effectively respond to assessment results by creating proficiency level descriptions, developing a range of quality assessment items aligned to those proficiency levels, setting mastery cut scores, and finally, improving grading practices.

How to facilitate the development of common formative assessments in small schools or when teachers do not share teaching assignments is the focus of Adam Young's chapter on "Using Common Assessments in Uncommon Courses." Adam shows how a collaborative focus on student learning can be used as a basis for building common formative assessments. He also describes an in-depth case study conducted in a small rural high school to illustrate how the process can work in the lives of busy classroom teachers.

Ainsley Rose's chapter on "Creating Equity in Classroom Assessment for English Language Learners and Students With Special Needs" takes on the challenge of developing alternative assessment formats that maintain the integrity of assessment principles. Emphasizing issues of fairness and equity, he describes several strategies for creating assessments that provide valuable information on the learning of English language learners as well as those in bilingual education programs, students with special needs, and gifted and talented students.

Part Three turns attention to the importance of "Involving Students in Assessment." It begins with Jeffry Overlie's chapter on "Creating Confident, Capable Learners," in which he stresses that involving students in assessments must become the rule rather the exception in modern classrooms. Jeffry then presents several self-assessment models that can be transferred to any classroom setting as a means to involve students in the assessment process.

Next, Nicole Vagle shares the results from studies on student involvement in "Inspiring and Requiring Action." Stressing that student involvement requires a sensitive combination of encouragement and pressure, she shares a variety of practical strategies for using descriptive feedback and error analysis to bring in students as partners on their learning journey.

In "Engaging the Nintendo Generation," Sharon Kramer and Linda DuBose present research on the importance of helping students understand where they are in the learning process, where they are going, and how to get there. They then provide a host of classroom strategies that teachers can implement immediately to involve students more purposefully in assessment activities.

We conclude with Tom Hierck's chapter, "Differentiated Pathways to Success." Tom argues that teachers who collect data on student learning through formative assessments and combine those data with other information they have about students create learning opportunities that can help all students succeed. He then takes the ideas of individualization and differentiation one step further, suggesting that we must ensure the success of every student in our charge if we are to move forward as a society.

In reading these chapters, some of you may find the different vocabulary and terminology used by the authors to be a bit confusing. What some authors call *targets* others call *anchors*, or *benchmarks*, or *steps*. What some label *criteria* others refer to as *proficiency levels* or *learning progressions*. What some authors describe as *unpacking* others consider *unwrapping* or *deconstructing*. And while some authors consider levels of mastery and proficiency to be the same, others view them as quite different.

Although it would be easy to be put off by this disparity in terminology, I urge you to look beyond these differences. The ideas these authors describe are far more important than the vocabulary that they use (Guskey, 2003). So please do not let these minor discrepancies in terminology distract you from the importance of each author's message. If necessary, simply translate the authors' words to fit the vocabulary that you and the educators with whom you work use. Distinctions in terminology are helpful when they facilitate communication, but they should never present barriers to our understanding of important ideas.

In addition, some of you may be distressed by the complicated nature of the issues involved and the lack of consistency in the authors' responses to these issues. In the midst of these differences, however, I believe you will be impressed by the insights the authors offer, the diversity of their perspectives on improvement, and the creativity and breadth of their proposed solutions. Taking full advantage of the benefits of assessment *for* learning requires not a single set of strategies or activities, but rather a range of strategies and activities—formal and informal—that must be adapted to the unique contextual characteristics of a classroom. What works in one setting may not work equally well in another. Instead, teachers must adapt strategies and activities to individual classroom contexts where a particular teacher teaches particular students from particular communities. Teachers who work in different contexts have unique needs that must be addressed in unique ways. Just as a "one size fits all" approach does not work with all students, it does not work with all teachers, either.

The hope that the authors of these chapters and I share is that the ideas and strategies presented on these pages will spur you to action. Given the recognized power of formative assessments to help improve student learning, we cannot wait for their slow and gradual evolution into modern classrooms. Far too many students will be lost if we do, abandoned by an educational system that holds the key to their success but does not use it. Instead, we need teacher leaders who press hard for broad-based implementation, armed with the established knowledge base of effective practice. Although the precise path each teacher takes in these challenging endeavors may be different, we believe that such action is absolutely necessary in order to ensure that all students learn well and gain the many positive benefits of that success. Our hope is that this book provides guidance to those willing to take on that challenge.

References

Black, P., & Wiliam, D. (1998). Inside the black box: Raising standards through classroom assessment. *Phi Delta Kappan, 80*(2), 139–144.

Bloom, B. S. (1971). Mastery learning. In J. H. Block (Ed.), *Mastery learning: Theory and practice* (pp. 47–63). New York: Holt, Rinehart & Winston.

Bloom, B. S., Hastings, J. T., & Madaus, G. (1971). *Handbook on formative and summative evaluation of student learning.* New York: McGraw-Hill.

Bloom, B. S., Madaus, G. F., & Hastings, J. T. (1981). *Evaluation to improve learning.* New York: McGraw-Hill.

Guskey, T. R. (2003). How classroom assessments improve learning. *Educational Leadership*, *60*(5), 6–11.

Guskey, T. R. (Ed.). (2006). *Benjamin S. Bloom: Portraits of an educator.* Lanham, MD: Rowman & Littlefield Education.

Guskey, T. R. (2007). Formative classroom assessment and Benjamin S. Bloom: Theory, research, and practice. In J. H. McMillan (Ed.), *Formative classroom assessment: Theory into practice* (pp. 63–78). New York: Teachers College.

Guskey, T. R. (2008). The rest of the story. *Educational Leadership*, *65*(4), 28–35.

Stiggins, R. (2008). *An introduction to student-involved assessment FOR learning* (5th ed.). Upper Saddle River, NJ: Merrill, Prentice Hall.

PART ONE

Laying the Foundation of Assessment Literacy

CASSANDRA ERKENS

An independent consultant and recognized leader in education, Cassandra Erkens shares her knowledge with teachers and administrators throughout the United States and Canada. She is the president of Anam Cara Consulting, Inc., and an adjunct faculty member at Hamline University, where she offers Master of Arts in Education courses and facilitates a learning community for educators engaged in the two-year MAEd extended degree program. Cassandra has served as a high school English teacher, district-level director of staff development, and state-level educational effectiveness regional facilitator. She is author and coauthor of several formal education-based training programs and contributed chapters to *The Principal as Assessment Leader* (Solution Tree, 2009), *The Collaborative Administrator: Working Together as a Professional Learning Community* (Solution Tree, 2008), and *The Collaborative Teacher: Working Together as a Professional Learning Community* (Solution Tree, 2008).

ONE

Developing Our Assessment Literacy

Cassandra Erkens

The discovery that few educators consider themselves to be "assessment literate" is startlingly consistent. When asked about their preparation in this area, "most teachers say they develop their assessment knowledge and practices on the job" (Topolka Jorissen, 2006, p. 22). And given how powerful we know assessment to be in the learning process, our lack of assessment literacy is consistently startling. How is it that teachers are not provided with the necessary formal instruction and practice to become skilled in designing and using quality assessments to support learning? In our undergraduate education programs, many of us received very little information or skill development regarding the accurate design and effective use of classroom assessments. Armed with little but our personal experiences, we then went into our classrooms, closed the doors, and developed our own assessment practices and beliefs, often re-creating the very limited or misinformed assessment experiences we ourselves navigated as learners.

Today, a strong case can be made that our profession has exchanged the development of our own assessment literacy for a reliance on the expertise of both textbook and testing companies (Popham, 2001; R. Stiggins, personal communication, May 21, 2008). We have trusted those we believe to be more knowledgeable in test-item development and statistical validity and reliability to develop our assessments. And we are right: textbook and testing companies *have* become much more assessment literate as they constantly field-test and improve their own questions and ultimately refine their craft knowledge and skills. However, we have erred in our understanding of the overall strengths, limitations, and even purposes of such assessments. We complain about their shortcomings, yet we easily employ these predesigned assessments in classrooms, and we accept their results as outside validation of our programs and efforts. So the problem isn't that those we have engaged for assessment development have failed in their task; the assessments that textbook and testing companies have designed have accomplished exactly what they are capable of accomplishing. But we have exaggerated the *value* of such assessments and used their data inappropriately (Popham, 2001; Popham, 2008a; R. Stiggins, personal communication, May 21, 2008). At the same time, we have misunderstood the significance and hence slighted the purpose of daily classroom assessment.

While it is true that our culture is filled with external accountability tests that are "instructionally insensitive" (Lederman & Burnstein, 2006; Popham, 2003, 2008b), many classroom assessments share some of that insensitivity. Today, for example, teacher-created tests often align more tightly with textbook content than state standards; the learning targets of the test items are not articulated such that teachers and learners can identify which targets the learner has mastered and which not; and the intentional scaffolding of the learning targets leading up to the test (that is, repeated opportunities for practice, from homework leading to test mastery) is abbreviated such that the power of corrective, descriptive feedback to alter instruction or promote continued learning is circumvented. By our own admission, we have created an imbalanced system skewed toward summative assessments. In doing so, we have limited the function of assessment to helping us identify what our students have mastered at a given point in time, and we have missed the opportunity to spend as much, if not *more*, time finding the answers to how we can help students advance.

As it turns out, assessment is *integral* to instruction (Black, Harrison, Lee, Marshall, & Wiliam, 2004; Heritage, 2007; Popham, 2003, 2008b; Stiggins & Chappuis, 2006; Stiggins, Chappuis, Chappuis, & Arter, 2007; Wiliam, 2007; Wiliam & Thompson, 2008). If we continue to provide instruction without attending to ongoing and in-the-moment assessment data, we will waste invaluable time with misfired instructional efforts and, worse, fail to support our students who depend on us to help them achieve mastery. In his July 2008 keynote address to the Portland, Oregon, assessment conference, assessment expert Richard Stiggins stated that assessment practice as we know it today is as much the cause of our current achievement gap as it is the potential solution to close that gap quickly.

Fortunately, we do know what quality looks like, because master teachers lead the way and provide the examples of quality we now know to replicate in using assessment and instruction practices to impact learning in powerful and positive ways (Wiliam & Thompson, 2008). However, the evidence that what we are doing *systemically* isn't working, coupled with the research on best practices in assessment design and use, fosters the overwhelmingly convincing argument that we *must* develop our assessment literacy. We can no longer neglect such a significant component of the teaching and learning process in the hopes that the expertise of textbook and testing companies will suffice.

What Is Assessment Literacy?

Assessment literacy can be defined as the state or quality of being knowledgeable and skilled in the comprehensive picture of assessment preparation and practice—categorized by Stiggins as the "accurate design" of assessment tools and the "effective use" of corresponding assessment responses (Stiggins, Chappuis, Chappuis, & Arter, 2007). To be assessment literate is to have the necessary knowledge, skills, and dispositions regarding the full array of assessment processes that will both monitor and promote our students' mastery of the learning expectations. It means being able to do the following:

- Create a formative culture and balanced assessment system conducive to learning.

- Identify the comprehensive and specific targets of rigorous and relevant learning expectations.

- Design accurate assessments to generate evidence that will sufficiently reflect the expectations.

- Employ in-the-moment, strategic prompts and questions to elicit reasoning and knowledge construction responses from learners.

- Deliver assessments in a safe and engaging environment.

- Analyze results from assessments.

- Respond accordingly to results from assessments with corrective feedback and responsive instruction.

- Reassess to verify learning and repeating the process as needed.

- Engage students as instructional decision makers in meaningful ways throughout the entire teaching and learning process.

Ultimately, when we are assessment literate, we monitor student responses to our instruction and assessment tasks, ask the right questions, cull through the responses we gather to find the learners *where they are,* and then work to *take them where they need to be.* We do this through dynamic, interactive instruction, appropriate feedback, and strategies that involve the learners as key decision makers in the process. And we persist in checking and rechecking along the way so we can continue the learning progression and know when each learner has "arrived" at mastery.

Clearly, there is much to understand about the role of assessment in the teaching and learning process. We must galvanize our own learning journey to address the gap between where we are now and where we would like to be with our assessment practice. As we now understand from the research on formative assessment (Black et al., 2004; Stiggins & Chappuis, 2006; Stiggins et al., 2007; Wiliam, 2007; Wiliam & Thompson, 2008), students in our classrooms learn by working their way through three critical and personally engaging questions:

1. Where am I going?

2. Where am I now?

3. How can I begin to address the gap?

As learners addressing our institutional gaps in assessment literacy, we must frame our work around the same three questions.

Where Are We Going?

To begin, it will be important for us to expand our understanding of assessment beyond the traditional understanding of *test*. Assessment is more than simply a pre-test, a quiz in the middle of the unit, a homework assignment, or a test at the end of a unit. Dylan Wiliam and Marnie Thompson want us to realize that "everything students do, such as conversing in groups, completing seatwork, answering questions, asking questions, working on projects, handing in homework assignments—even sitting silently and looking confused—is a potential source of information about what they do and do not understand" (2007, p. 5).

Rick Stiggins, Steve Chappuis, Jan Chappuis, and Judith Arter (2007) suggest that assessment—summative *or* formative—involves the gathering of data that will enable us to make decisions: what can students and teachers alike do to support continued learning (formative), and what has the student already mastered at a given point in time (summative)? Assessment experts sound the call for us to create a balanced assessment system of summative and formative assessments that will move beyond monitoring student learning into promoting and enhancing continued learning.

Understanding assessment is not as simple as adhering to a set of rules such as the following:

- Summative assessments can only be used to monitor student learning, and formative assessments can only be used to promote student learning.

- Only score summative assessments.

- Never score formative assessments.

However, if we keep the formative question, How can I help you learn more? at the core of our efforts to design and use assessments, we should be able to make informed decisions that benefit learners. Rules, by their very nature, create situations and/or environments that cannot be sensitive to individuals' needs. To create an instructionally sensitive learning environment, teachers need guidelines—founded in best-practice research—that can accommodate changing contexts. The context in which teachers operate matters; the standards, the strategies, the culture, the teacher's strengths, and especially the students themselves, create variables that *require* teachers to be masters of their craft because a single set of rules or "one size fits all" approach will not meet the needs of our diverse learners. If we understand what we are trying to accomplish instructionally with *each learner*, however, we can use the assessment process to leverage the outcome. We might not handle each situation in exactly the same way with exactly the same prescribed activities, responses, or solutions. In addition to offering specific corrective feedback, we may, for example, provide a score on a formative assessment as a means to help learners see the gap between where they are and where they need to be—but we may not include that "benchmark" score in the final body of evidence used to determine grades. Wiliam highlights the importance of being grounded in the research so that we can engage in sophisticated, expert decision making regarding our practice: "That is why 'what works' is not the right question in education. Everything works somewhere, and nothing works everywhere" (2006, p. 17).

When we are firm in our understanding of the research, we can guide our instruction and assessment practice in integrated and informed ways. We do not teach because we love the art of providing information in interesting ways; we teach because we want to promote learning. When we embed that commitment for learning into helping *all* learners be successful, it becomes instantly apparent that assessment and instruction are integrated, and one size can never fit all. As we consider our direction with assessment, we must acknowledge that we have room to address our own gap in understanding and leveraging the power of formative assessments.

The clarion call to balance our system with far more formative assessments is compelling. However, it is only one part of where we need to go with changes in our assessment practices. Equally important, we must acknowledge that the shift from an industrial age to an information age will demand a change in the purpose and structure of the assessments we must design. Where once the scarcity of print resources required schools to help learners gather and retain information, now the abundance of electronic resources will require schools to help learners navigate, manage, and create information with fidelity (Weinberger, 2007). It will be a grave disservice to our students if we continue our assessment practice of having students "give back" the content and processes they learned so we can observe mastery. Futurist David Weinberger contends that in a digital world where knowledge is freed from two-dimensional constraints, information becomes miscellaneous, and "the solution to the overabundance of information is more information" as we organize and sort data for new insights and understandings (2007, p. 13). Our assessments must begin to monitor for what students can *do* with information.

According to Fred Newmann, M. Bruce King, and Dana Carmichael (2007), we cannot prepare our students for the future by simply providing more instruction on reasoning skills or strategies for information literacy; instead, our assessments must exact "authentic intellectual work." To do this, we must move the challenge for our learners from "complying with teachers' and tests' requirements" to demonstrating the "original application of knowledge and skills" in "complex and socially or personally meaningful work" (p. 3). Our assessments must become far more demanding as learners engage in disciplined inquiry to construct new knowledge in authentic contexts. In a ubiquitous, global, and hyperlinked learning environment—which is growing regardless of the status of our technological readiness—it is entirely possible for students to solve authentic problems in genuine and publishable ways.

How might that look? The following assessment is traditional in its approach: it elicits reasoning through written communication, and it requires students to share what they have learned by activating their memory and recording what they retrieve on fresh notebook paper:

> You need to choose one of the law proposals that we have discussed in class. You can either agree with that law proposal or disagree with it. The essay can be written from either side. It is a four-paragraph essay. The essay should be written in your notebook, starting on a fresh page. You will need to tear it out of your notebook to hand it in. [The assignment goes on to clarify what each paragraph in the essay is charged with accomplishing.]

If we used assessment to monitor for authentic intellectual work, the task would more likely engage students in using information as a point of reference for arriving at plausible solutions to a real issue:

> Our student news station has been reporting a growing awareness of and concern about bullying in our school. *Using the context and the insights gathered from at least two of the laws we have studied in class*, develop a law that you believe will address the issue and create a safe learning

environment for our diverse student population. In addition to stating your proposed law, be sure to provide the rationale for your law, the process you would use to develop and pass such a law, and your recommended enforcements of that law.

Using a rubric aligned with the criteria of authentic intellectual work, we'd then score the students' work, monitoring for clear, reasoned, and accurate communications that demonstrate an exemplary understanding of the social studies concepts applied to new contexts (Newmann, King, & Carmichael, 2007). If the mission of schools is to prepare our students to be successful, wise, contributing members of the world in which they'll live, we must consider the demands of the future. In our own uncertain future, we have some known certainties: "We are currently preparing students for jobs that don't yet exist using technologies that haven't yet been invented in order to solve problems we don't even know we have" (Melsa, 2007, p. 56). And in such a context, with the looming reality that the rate of information is doubling faster than we can produce new books, we must redirect our assessment efforts to be less about restating what was learned and more about developing the minds needed for such a world. In his book *Five Minds for the Future,* Howard Gardner has identified the disciplinary mind, the synthesizing mind, the creating mind, the respectful mind, and the ethical mind as the cognitive, global, and human capacities that are now at a premium and will be even more so in a rapidly changing world; he asserts that if we are to "meet the new world on its own terms, we should begin to cultivate these capacities now" (2006, p. 2).

Our work with assessment brings to life our educational aspirations. As we work to hone our assessment literacy, we cannot limit our efforts to changing the *how* of assessment design and use today; we must consider the challenges our learners will face in a dynamic and diverse tomorrow.

Where Are We Now?

In any meaningful change effort, we must conduct a reality check on "what is." What are our current assessment practices? Do they support learning? More pointedly, what do we believe about learning? How does it happen? What does it take to make it happen, and how can assessment help both teacher and learner along the way? Does our current practice of *assess/score/move to next unit* promote progressive learning opportunities and profound understanding? Our answers to these questions reveal our beliefs about learning, but they may also reveal how our beliefs do not necessarily align with our current assessment practices. In fact, some of our assessment practices today might be regarded as the unthinking application of past precedents. In order to move forward, we must first identify some of our own fallacies, especially those that block us from a more formative orientation.

Fallacy: Faster Is Smarter

When we say things like, "But I want to reward the students who got it right the first time with the better grades," we operate on the premise that the students who learn things quickly are the smarter students. While most educators believe that making mistakes is an inherent part of the learning journey, popular classroom practice penalizes mistakes (for example, by grading everything students submit). For some learners, a mistake indicates what *shouldn't be*, and once made, the mistake becomes the informative tool that actually promotes understanding and application of what *should be*. The learning that emerges from mistakes fixed as a result of proper corrective feedback can be so powerful that similar or repeated mistakes become unlikely as the student achieves a deeper understanding of the content and processes. For example, many of us confess that we made many mistakes in our first year (or years) of teaching that more quickly solidified for us what *not* to do and what *to do instead* than any pedagogical textbook or classroom discussion ever could. Mistakes, then, can be a valuable learning tool, but such a tool will never fare well in a system that is predicated on rewarding the right answers achieved earliest in the learning journey.

None of this is to suggest that we should celebrate mistakes. To do so would send the wrong message. But perhaps we could *leverage* mistakes without penalty and create the very learning opportunity that will engage learners and support their efforts to close the gap between where they are and where they need to be. Unfortunately, when we track errors made during learning in our gradebooks—even if we only record "number correct"— and then average grades at the end of a unit, we end up holding students accountable for the very mistakes that, once connected, may have launched their newfound level of mastery.

In her 2006 book *Mindset: The New Psychology of Success*, Carol Dweck indicates that challenged students with a "growth mindset" are ready to take risks, make mistakes, and apply effort to their learning with the belief that they will "get smarter" and be successful: "Not only weren't they discouraged by failure, they didn't even think they were failing. They thought they were learning" (p. 4). The assessment process as we know it can easily discourage risk taking. If we can release the idea that "faster is smarter" and design systems that allow for the true learning process of leveraging mistakes, then the assessment process has the power to motivate and excite, encourage learning, and foster a sense of resiliency and efficacy.

Fallacy: Quantity Lends Credence

Reporting our evaluation of another's work is scary; our professional judgment might be called into question. We have believed that if we had a large body of evidence from which to support our conclusions, our evaluations would be less suspect. We have used the average of thirty scores, for example, to assert with some level of confidence that student X consistently does C work. But there are glaring errors in our reasoning. To begin, when averaging, we deceive the public, ourselves, and most importantly, *the learner* regarding the true level of mastery achieved on the continuum of learning expectations. In *Classroom Assessment and Grading That Work*, Robert Marzano states, "Averaging assumes that no learning has occurred from assessment to assessment. . . . Learning theory and common sense tell us that a student might start a grading period with little or no knowledge regarding a topic but end the grading period with a great deal of knowledge" (2006, pp. 96–97). Such widespread patterns of treating all assessments as summative, grading them all, and then averaging those grades must ultimately force us to ask if our current assessment practices and expectations align with our beliefs about learning.

We can develop more credence in our scoring by reducing the quantity of scores but increasing the number of people— including the learner—who agree that the score we have identified is an accurate representation of the student's performance against a publicly approved set of criteria. When we engage our students in clarifying their learning expectations, co-creating rubrics of quality, using those rubrics on their work and the work of others (in and outside of the classroom), self-assessing, goal setting, self-monitoring, and self-reflecting, we can create mutual understanding and agreement. If we give up on scoring everything, we can find more time for providing the critical feedback that will encourage the growth we are seeking on behalf of our learners.

If we give up on averaging, we can step back and take a holistic view of the student's overall performance, watching for a growth trend line and identifying where the student ended in his or her mastery of our learning expectations.

Fallacy: Required *Trumps* Engaged

The premise that *required* is more important than *engaged* is evident in the kinds of work we assign. The fact that something is required is important, but that will not guarantee learning on the part of our students; as the adage says, "You can lead a horse to water, but you can't make him drink." "Required" generates compliance first and learning may (or may not) follow; "engaged" generates learning first (even when the experience can be frustrating for the learner), and then compliance follows. When our assessments are engaging, we almost can't *stop* learning from happening! Unfortunately, authors Linda Kaser and Judy Halbert (2008) summarize grim findings from the Programme for International Student Assessment (PISA):

> Observations in many intermediate and secondary class-rooms and interviews with learners indicate that many young people are under-engaged or disengaged with the learning opportunities in their schools. . . . The most recent PISA report suggests that close to half of all secondary learners across the countries studied are disengaged in school and are going through the motions of learning with an externally motivated, "performativity" habit of mind. (p. 56)

When things are required, students work to please teachers. When things are engaging, students work because it is pleasing. Few worksheets hit the mark of "engaging" for our students. While worksheets do serve a purpose, we might have an over-abundance of "worksheet learning." We must create assessments that require authentic intellectual work, for that will be engaging. Students are naturally curious and interested in solving the issues they face.

Our fallacy list could continue. The point is, if we believe that learning involves engaging in disciplined inquiry, constructing new knowledge, understanding oneself as a learner on a journey, *and* learning the value and the reward of effort, then we must more closely align our assessment practices with our true pedagogical beliefs.

What Can We Begin to Do to Close the Gap?

It might be easy to find books, graduate courses, or professional development workshops on the topic of assessment, and such opportunities are important in our efforts to build shared research-based knowledge. But simply *getting* the information will never suffice. We know a better way—working in communities and learning by doing. Noel Tichy, an author and expert in the field of leadership, states:

> To create organizations that get smarter and more aligned every day requires an interactive teaching/learning process. It isn't hierarchical teaching. You teach me, and then I teach the people below me. It isn't about alternating roles. You teach me something and then I'll teach you something. Rather, it is a process of mutual exploration and exchange during which both the "teacher" and the "learner" become smarter. It is synergy. 1 + 1 = 3. (2008, p. 10)

We must create and harness our own synergy around changing the assessment culture in which we conduct the life-giving business of *learning*.

We must engage in collective inquiry as we explore and enrich our understanding of assessment literacy. Together, we inquire into "1) best practices about teaching and learning, 2) a candid clarification of [our] current practices, and 3) an honest assessment of [our] students' current levels of learning" (DuFour, DuFour, & Eaker, 2008, p. 16). In community, we refine our thinking as we come to consensus, we examine our craft relative to a collective body of results from our direct application of the practices we are learning, and we support each other in the unforeseen challenges that emerge along the way.

If we are to debunk our own fallacies, there are important questions for us to explore. Using the process of action research, teaching teams generate compelling questions for which they crave answers. The options are limitless:

- How do I engage and motivate the elementary learner in self-assessment and self-reflection for his or her learning?

- How can I engage students in co-creating rubrics to use in peer review, personal goal setting, self-evaluation, and teacher evaluation?

- How can I differentiate homework assignments to target the specific learning needs of individual students?

- How can I create an environment where students readily enhance and support one another's learning?

- How can I develop a grading system that supports motivation for achievement in writing?

- How can I enhance my current art lessons with art criticism activities that stimulate deep thinking for secondary students?

With such questions in hand, teams decide what research-based strategies they will investigate and how they will measure the effectiveness of those strategies. The exploration and the shared findings tied to student achievement will inform and change practice faster than reading a book, trying a strategy independently, or attending a workshop ever could (Tichy, 2008; Stiggins, Chappuis, Chappuis, & Arter, 2007; DuFour, DuFour, & Eaker, 2008; Wiliam & Thompson, 2008).

One of the best ways to address our team's assessment literacy is to identify and share success criteria for our work (Wiliam, 2006). Establishing criteria helps to fortify the targets of our learning and clarify quality applications of our work. When we develop a rubric for quality assessments, we give ourselves a tool with which to have candid conversations grounded in research-based expectations as we examine current practice. If, for example, we were to adopt or modify rubrics for Stiggins' five keys to designing accurate assessments and using them effectively (Stiggins et al., 2007), we could use the tool to examine the quality of our own assessments. Are the targets clear? Will we generate enough of a sampling of student learning for each target? Are the questions or assessment processes biased in any way? When we do this work together, we naturally begin to push on one another's thinking: *Do we really need thirty-five questions aimed at the concept of slope? Will this question elicit reasoning and clarify student understanding?* The rich discussions that ensue solidify our understanding of assessment and move us toward application and systems alignment. Moreover, the rubric becomes a measure to hold us accountable to that which we say we value and desire.

In addition to examining our current assessment products and practices, we begin designing new ones. Again, the best approach is collaboration, as we co-create, creatively problem solve, share strategies, monitor student learning, and hold one another accountable to our standards for excellence along the way. As classroom teachers, we give teaching our best shot the first time we teach. If our best shot did not work the first time, and a "louder and slower" version of the same approach rarely works the second time, then we will have to help one another find alternatives. When we "[1] analyze, understand, and deconstruct standards, 2) transform standards into high-quality classroom assessments, and 3) share and interpret the results together" (Stiggins, 2005, p. 82), we benefit from our collective wisdom about how to continue to promote student learning. This work is challenging. We will have more confidence in our results, our evaluation of the findings, and our planned responses to the findings when we work with trusted colleagues.

Working in community, we must collaboratively score student work. As we define our expectations for learners, we must come to a shared understanding of what quality looks like. It can take a long time to write a rubric as a team, but even that is not sufficient. Team members who agree on rubric language will still end up scoring their own student papers differently unless they have the opportunity to practice together. An additional benefit of practicing is that it helps us refine the language of the rubric itself, and it provides us with anchor papers for future work and exemplars to share with our students. The greatest benefit of all in collaborating to score student work is that we increase our assessment literacy along the way. According to Linda Darling-Hammond and her colleagues, "Studies have found that teachers who are involved in scoring performance assessments with other colleagues and discussing their students' work report the experience helped them change their practice to become more problem-oriented and more diagnostic" (Darling-Hammond et al., 2008, p. 208). Our focused, engaged, and collaborative discussions will help us move theory into practice.

Learning is risky business—for both adult and student learners:

> To learn is to risk; to lead others toward profound levels of learning is to risk; to promote personal and organizational renewal is to risk. To create schools hospitable to human learning is to risk. In short, the career of the lifelong learner and of the school-based reformer is the life of a risk-taker. (Barth, 2001, p. 187)

Ignoring the amount of risk learning entails for students *and* for ourselves as educators will have lifelong, dire consequences. In her research on organizational change and creating learning organizations, Amy Edmondson has found that

> psychological safety is crucial, especially in organizations where knowledge constantly changes, where workers need to collaborate, and where those workers must make wise decisions without management intervention. It's built on the premise that no one can perform perfectly in every situation when knowledge and best practice are moving targets. (2008, p. 63)

The work before us is challenging. It also presents exciting opportunities to engage in our own authentic intellectual work and to learn collaboratively—the same opportunities we want to give our students. To alter our assessment practices, we will have to collectively develop our collective assessment literacy. While we can never truly "arrive" at mastery, we can most certainly come closer as we promote continued learning for our students and ourselves.

References

Barth, R. (2001). *Learning by heart.* San Francisco: Jossey-Bass.

Black, P., Harrison, C., Lee, C., Marshall, B., & Wiliam, D. (2004). Working inside the black box: Assessment for learning in the classroom. *Phi Delta Kappan, 86*(1), 9–21.

Darling-Hammond, L., Barron, B., Pearson, P. D., Schoenfeld, A. H., Stage, E. K., Zimmerman, T. D., et al. (2008). *Powerful learning: What we know about teaching for understanding.* San Francisco: Jossey-Bass.

DuFour, R., DuFour, R., & Eaker, R. (2008). *Revisiting professional learning communities at work: New insights for improving schools.* Bloomington, IN: Solution Tree.

Dweck, C. (2006). *Mindset: The new psychology of success.* New York: Random House.

Edmondson, A. C. (2008, July/August). The competitive imperative of learning. *Harvard Business Review, 86*(7/8), 60–67.

Gardner, H. (2006). *Five minds for the future.* Boston: Harvard Business School.

Heritage, M. (2007, October). Formative assessment: What do teachers need to know and do? *Phi Delta Kappan, 89*(2), 140–145.

Kaser, L., & Halbert, J. (2008). From sorting to learning: Developing deep learning in Canadian schools. *Education Canada, 48*(5), 56–59.

Lederman, L. M., & Burnstein, R. A. (2006, February). Alternative approaches to high-stakes testing. *Phi Delta Kappan, 87*(6), 429–432.

Marzano, R. (2006). *Classroom assessment and grading that work.* Alexandria, VA: Association for Supervision and Curriculum Development.

Melsa, J. L. (2007). The forces driving change: President's letter. *ASEE Prism, 17*(1), 55–56.

Newmann, F. M., King, M. B., & Carmichael, D. L. (2007). *Authentic instruction and assessment: Common standards for rigor and relevance in teaching*. Des Moines: Iowa Department of Education.

Popham, W. J. (2001). *The truth about testing: An educator's call to action*. Alexandria, VA: Association for Supervision and Curriculum Development.

Popham, W. J. (2003). *Test better, teach better: The instructional role of assessment*. Alexandria, VA: Association for Supervision and Curriculum Development.

Popham, W. J. (2008a). Classroom assessment: Staying instructionally afloat in an ocean of accountability. In C. A. Dwyer (Ed.), *The future of assessment: Shaping teaching and learning* (pp. 263–278). New York: Lawrence Erlbaum Associates.

Popham, W. J. (2008b). *Transformative assessment*. Alexandria, VA: Association for Supervision and Curriculum Development.

Stiggins, R. (2005). Assessment for learning: Building a culture of confident learners. In R. DuFour, R. Eaker, & R. DuFour (Eds.), *On common ground: The power of professional learning communities* (pp. 65–83). Bloomington, IN: Solution Tree (formerly National Educational Service).

Stiggins, R. (2008, July 16). *Assessment FOR learning and the achievement gap*. Keynote address presented at the Educational Testing Service annual assessment conference, Portland, OR.

Stiggins, R., & Chappuis, J. (2006, Winter). What a difference a word makes: Assessment FOR learning rather than assessment OF learning helps students succeed. *Journal of Staff Development, 27*(1), 10–14.

Stiggins, R., Chappuis, S., Chappuis, J., & Arter, J. (2007). *Classroom assessment* for *student learning: Doing it right—Using it well*. Portland, OR: ETS Assessment Training Institute.

Tichy, N. (2008). *The cycle of leadership: How great leaders teach their companies to win*. New York: Harper Business.

Topolka Jorissen, K. (2006, Winter). Three skillful moves to assessment for the busy principal. *Journal of Staff Development, 27*(1), 22–30.

Weinberger, D. (2007). *Everything is miscellaneous: The power of the new digital order*. New York: Times Books.

Wiliam, D. (2006, Winter). Assessment: Learning communities can use it to engineer a bridge connecting teaching and learning. *Journal of Staff Development, 27*(1), 16–20.

Wiliam, D. (2007, December/2008, January). Changing classroom practice. *Educational Leadership, 65*(4), 36–42.

Wiliam, D., & Thompson, M. (2007, April). *Tight but loose: A conceptual framework for scaling up school reforms.* Paper presented at the annual meeting of the American Educational Research Association, Chicago, IL. Accessed at www.dylanwiliam.net on September 30, 2008.

Wiliam, D., & Thompson, M. (2008). Integrating assessment with learning: What will it take to make it work? In C. A. Dwyer (Ed.), *The future of assessment: Shaping teaching and learning* (pp. 53–82). New York: Lawrence Erlbaum Associates.

CHRIS JAKICIC

 Chris Jakicic, EdD, has worked as an adjunct instructor at National-Louis University as well as Loyola University Chicago, where she earned her doctorate of education. She is the former principal of Woodlawn Middle School in Long Grove, Illinois, where she guided the staff toward a collaborative culture focused on learning and assessment *for* learning practices. Teachers began collaborating to write common assessments, engaging students in self-assessment, and making grades more transparent. Dr. Jakicic then designed a one-day workshop for all middle school teachers in the district to train them about why writing and using common assessments is so essential. She has published articles in the *Journal of Staff Development* and *Illinois School Research and Development Journal* and is a contributor to *The Principal as Assessment Leader* (Solution Tree, 2009) and *The Collaborative Teacher: Working Together as a Professional Learning Community* (Solution Tree, 2008).

TWO

Assessment That Makes Sense

Chris Jakicic

Across North America, teachers are responding to the over-whelming research about the important role formative assessment plays in measuring and monitoring student learning. However, many teachers are still stymied by how they can use formative assessment data in their classrooms to help develop daily lesson plans. In fact, many teachers believe that we are testing too much—that they already know which students will do poorly on assessments (even before administering them) and that the results of assessments don't provide the information they need to make decisions about what to teach next. The premise of this chapter is that the reason teachers feel this way is that they are using the wrong types of assessments to get the feedback they need. They may be relying too heavily on summative assessments and may not have enough formative ones. So, with some simple changes in assessment development, teachers will be able to respond quickly to students who aren't learning, because they will have the information they need to do so.

It is hard to find an educational journal or book written recently that doesn't acknowledge the strong connection between using the results of frequent, formative assessment and improved student learning. The most widely cited research in this area comes from Paul Black and Dylan Wiliam's 1998 summary and meta-analysis of the international research around formative assessment. When they examined 250 studies, they concluded that schools could expect a .4 to .7 standard deviation gain in student achievement as a result of using frequent, formative assessments. This is a significant improvement, and teachers are trying to ensure that they are doing whatever it takes to boost the achievement of their students.

At the same time, more schools are failing to meet AYP (adequate yearly progress) standards for all students as the expectations increase every year (Hoff, 2008). As a result, educators face a love-hate relationship with assessments; they see the importance of testing and yet feel the sting of punishment for failure to meet high-stakes expectations for all their students' learning. When educators understand that data are the key to knowing what to teach next, and when they learn how to use high-stakes summative assessment data more effectively and to gather more data with frequent, teacher-created, formative assessments, they can overcome their fears about assessment.

Gathering Data That Make Sense

The effective use of assessment data starts with laying out an assessment system that ensures that teachers get the information they need from their assessments. A balanced assessment system includes both assessment *of* learning, or summative assessment, and assessment *for* learning, formative assessment.

Summative Data

It is not uncommon for teachers to get back the results of their state tests and go through a process of data analysis to uncover strengths and weaknesses. They want to identify students with learning gaps and to remediate those deficiencies in their classrooms. Teachers will often make a list of all of the students who failed to meet expectations and then wonder what to do next. In an effort to use the information, they will try to disaggregate their results (break down specific data points) by standard. Unfortunately, they will most likely become more frustrated or less confident the more they dig into the data, because these tests don't provide sufficient information about each learning target for teachers to use for student remediation. In discussing how state test results are reported, James Popham (2008/2009, p. 85) says, "But the tests, and their resultant reports, were not conceptualized from the get-go to provide instructionally actionable data. And they don't." State tests are typically designed around state standards. These standards are often broken down into grade-level expectations or performance standards. However, when we examine them carefully, we find that even these expectations are written in broad strokes. For example, a grade-level expectation in California for sixth-grade math is: "Solve problems involving addition, subtraction, multiplication and division of positive fractions and explain why a particular operation was used for a given situation" (*Mathematics Content Standards for CA Public Schools*, n.d., p. 26). Even if the data from the state assessment give the teacher a list of students who failed this expectation, the teacher has little guidance to know exactly why each student failed. Did the student not know any of the operations with fractions? Did he or she fail one operation? When the teacher looks further, she may find out that there were only two or three questions used to measure this expectation—hardly enough to provide information about what the student didn't know!

This is not to suggest that there isn't a valid purpose for the summative data. It simply means that when teachers try to use those data in a formative way, they will experience difficulty. Understanding the difference between these two types of assessments is key to knowing better how to use the data that result from each. Summative assessments occur at the end of a unit or course and summarize what the students learned or didn't learn. They are intended to be used for giving grades and measuring the overall learning of students against a given standard. State tests are summative. The results tell teachers how well their instructional strategies worked in general and whether their pacing was appropriate but don't tell them what did or didn't work for a particular student. As Larry Ainsworth and Donald Viegut (2006, p. 24) explain:

> As all instruction and related learning activities for the particular standards have concluded, the results of summative assessments are not used to improve student understanding for *current* students. Instead, teachers typically use these assessment results to judge the effectiveness of their teaching practices and to improve instruction of those standards for *future* students.

So, if teachers can't effectively use these assessments to tell them what to teach next in their classrooms, is there a worthwhile purpose for them? Because state test results often lead to punitive results for schools whose student populations don't meet expectations, teachers tend to view them negatively. However, schools, teams, and teachers can in fact use the results of these assessments very effectively.

Summative assessments, including state tests, provide teachers with information that can be used to examine effective teaching strategies, pacing guidelines, and curriculum strengths and weaknesses. These assessments provide the data we need to measure whether we are meeting our goals. In fact, it is often these assessments that teachers should look to first to focus their team goals.

Analyzing Patterns

When working with summative assessments, look for patterns in the data. Jan O'Neill and Anne Conzemius (2006) explain that schools should first decide what is their greatest area of need. This is determined by looking at the summative assessments for the school and deciding which subject area has the lowest scores as well as which subject area shows the least amount of improvement over time, that is, the area that is not making progress from one year to the next. Teachers often find that graphing their test results will help them see the patterns in their data. For example, if a teacher team examined the state test data in table 2.1, the teachers would notice that for 2007, the lowest percentages of students proficient were in the areas of reading and science.

Table 2.1: Percentage of Students Meeting State Proficiency Standards

	2004	2005	2006	2007
Math	36	43	52	68
Writing	43	53	62	67
Reading	63	65	67	63
Science	45	48	60	61

If they graphed the results, they would see the pattern depicted in figure 2.1.

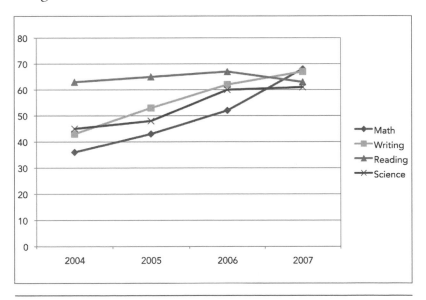

Figure 2.1: The graphed results of state assessments by percentage of students meeting standards.

In deciding what area they would focus on as a school for the following year, they would notice that while all of the 2007 percentages of proficiency are within 7 points of each other, reading percentages have made the least progress. While science proficiency percentages are currently the lowest, the team would likely pick reading as the greatest area of need because it doesn't appear that what teachers are currently doing is helping to improve student achievement. Keep in mind that this process is not about using summative assessments to look at individual or groups of students, but rather to help evaluate the effectiveness of curriculum, instruction, and pacing decisions.

The next step is to look more closely at these data to see what other information they can provide. Many states break the data from each subject area into the standards they've identified for that grade level. Thus, the reading data are likely to be broken down further into information about word analysis, comprehension of informational text, literary analysis, and so on. These disaggregated data help teachers to develop a more accurate plan to improve achievement. Consider the data in table 2.2.

Table 2.2: Disaggregated State Assessment Results in Reading by Percentage of Students Meeting Proficiency Standards

	2004	2005	2006	2007
Word Analysis	63	66	69	62
Comprehension (Informational Text)	57	59	56	52
Literary Analysis	69	70	76	75

When looking for patterns in these data, the team would notice that higher percentages of students were proficient in literary analysis than in comprehension of informational text. The teachers should note that proficiency percentages in literary analysis are improving while those in comprehension of informational text are declining. Based on this, team members will want to create an action plan that emphasizes instruction in comprehension of informational text. They will also want to make sure they continue to use the strategies they have been using that seem to be helping students in the area of literary analysis.

SMART Goals

Mike Schmoker (1999, p. 24) explains the purpose of goals by saying that "goals and the commitment they generate are the glue that holds teams together." Team goals ensure that teachers will work interdependently to accomplish the results they've laid out. Teams write SMART goals—Strategic and Specific, Measurable, Attainable, Results-oriented, and Time-bound (O'Neill & Conzemius, 2006)—to ensure they focus on results rather than intentions. These goals also create a culture in which teachers are responsible for *all* the students on the team rather than only those students assigned to their classes.

As discussed previously, teams examine their summative assessments to determine their greatest area of need. Teams then use the data generated by subsequent summative assessments to measure the progress they've made toward accomplishing the goal.

Just as there are different purposes for summative and formative assessment data to guide instruction, there are different purposes for their use in goal setting. When initially setting the goal, teams should use their summative assessment data to determine which area is most important to focus on. However, since some summative assessments may occur only annually, teams would have to wait a whole year to know whether their strategies are producing successful results. Therefore, teams should develop interim assessments to monitor short-term results toward the learning targets.

Formative Assessment Data

What summative data do not give teachers is specific information about why certain students didn't meet proficiency standards and what to do next to help them. To get the information that will enable them to know what to do next in their classrooms, teachers will need frequent formative assessments.

Some schools will decide to have teachers work together in teams to write common formative assessments, while in other schools, teachers will be responsible for their own assessments. Whichever choice a school makes, it is important to remember that the purpose of these assessments is to provide teachers the information they need about how to respond to students as soon as they experience difficulty.

When they begin the process of writing formative assessments, teachers often ask two questions: (1) how are these assessments different from my current classroom assessments? and (2) how are these assessments different from the many ways I check for understanding with my students?

In regards to the first question, if a teacher's current practice follows the traditional model, she gives tests and quizzes that are intended to be summative. These assessments are given after the teacher has finished teaching the concept or unit and are used to give students a grade on what they've learned. Formative assessments, on the other hand, are intended to be given while the teacher is still teaching so that both teachers *and their students* know what has been learned and what help the students still need. They are designed to provide teachers information about whether students have learned what was taught and, if not, what they should do next to help. So, one shift in thinking takes place when teachers re-examine the purpose of their classroom assessments and see that formative assessments can provide more than information that leads only to a grade.

The second question—about how formative assessment is different from checking for understanding—often arises as teachers explore the variety of ways they can assess student progress beyond the traditional selected-response items on multiple-choice, true/false, and matching tests. Many of the instructional strategies that teachers have always used to check for understanding can be modified to provide formative information about student learning. For example, teachers commonly ask questions during direct instruction to determine if students are understanding the material. But they sometimes call on one student and assume that that student represents the whole group. Better strategies include having each student answer the question on a dry-erase board or having each student use four index cards labeled *A*, *B*, *C*, and *D* to answer multiple-choice questions (Leahy, Lyon, Thompson, & Wiliam, 2005). The teacher then knows which students, and how many, weren't able to answer the question. Heritage (2007) suggests that teachers gather information during the lesson by using "curriculum-embedded assessments" that are part of the regular classroom activities to inform their instruction. For example, she describes how a science notebook that students regularly keep can be used to determine if students have understood the new material. The notebook isn't used as a test or for a grade, but it tells the teacher *during the instructional process* what each of his or her students is learning. Another similar strategy is the use of exit slips, which ask students to respond to a few questions at the end of the lesson about the instruction that occurred that day. After reviewing the index cards, the teacher can decide whether the students are ready to move on or if they need additional instruction (Datnow, Park, & Kennedy, 2008).

Douglas Fisher and Nancy Frey (2007) describe a new technology that allows a teacher to ask the class a question and have students use clickers to send their responses to the teacher's computer, which then displays both individual and total class responses. Teachers have immediate feedback from all students. Another suggestion Fisher and Frey make is that student writing can be used both to find out what specific content students have learned in content-area classrooms and to determine what the next steps should be for teaching spelling, grammar, and reading comprehension in language arts classes.

Homework is another commonly used instructional strategy that can easily be used in a formative way. Susan Christopher (2007/2008) suggests that when used formatively, "homework becomes a safe place to try out new skills without penalty. . . . Effective homework is the rehearsal before the final event" (p. 74).

Creating Formative Assessments That Work

Sometimes it's hard to distinguish between good teaching practices and good assessment practices, particularly when looking at formative assessment. Popham (2008, p. 112) suggests the following definition: "Formative assessment is a planned process, in which assessment-elicited evidence of students' status is used by teachers to adjust their ongoing instructional procedures or by students to adjust their current learning tactics." If we accept Popham's definition, formative assessments are not improvised or spontaneous; rather, they are administered at a particular time in the teaching-learning process for the teacher to get feedback about how to proceed. While they do not have to be written as tests or quizzes to provide the necessary information, they do need to be structured in a way that gives the teacher specific information about whether the student has learned the concept that has just been taught and is able to integrate the new information into already-taught concepts. When an assessment is written around a standard or grade-level expectation, it will not provide information that is specific enough for the teacher to know what to do next.

Consider the teacher who is addressing the standard "Students will be able to solve problems requiring them to add fractions with like and unlike denominators." If the assessment includes a number of problems asking students to add fractions of different types, as would be expected on a summative assessment, teachers won't know why the students who failed the assessment did so. If, on the other hand, students are taught how to find the least common denominator and then assessed on this particular learning target, teachers know how to respond the next day to both the students who did learn it and those who didn't. Kim Marshall (2008) talks about creating assessments that will gather data that are the right "grain size." That is, the information teachers need from formative assessments must be specific enough to be able to tell them what to do next in their classrooms. By writing assessments around the targets from deconstructed standards, teachers will get data that are the right grain size.

Determine What to Assess

The first step in planning assessments, then, is for teachers to deconstruct their standards into the individual learning targets that students will need to meet. Deconstructing begins as teachers determine what *type* of standard they are working with. Rick Stiggins, Judith Arter, Jan Chappuis, and Stephen Chappuis (2004) identify four types of standards: (1) knowledge and understanding, (2) reasoning, (3) performance, and (4) product standards. *Knowledge standards* ask students to know about something or explain what it means. *Reasoning standards* ask students to use information to solve problems. *Performance standards* ask students to follow a process to complete a task. *Product standards* require students to create a product. Once teachers identify the type of standard, they will understand what types of learning targets are likely embedded in the standard. Typically, knowledge standards only have knowledge targets; reasoning standards have knowledge and reasoning targets; performance standards have knowledge, reasoning, and performance targets; and product standards have product, performance, reasoning, and knowledge targets.

Teachers will thus identify our example standard, "Students will be able to solve problems requiring them to add fractions with like and unlike denominators," as a reasoning standard. They will then know that this standard will have knowledge and reasoning targets. Prior to designing formative assessments, they will need to determine what targets are embedded in the standard and what targets they will assess. Targets might include:

- Students will identify the numerator and a denominator in a fraction.

- Students will understand why fractions must have the same denominator to add together.

- Students will find the least common denominator (LCD) for several fractions.

- Students will find equivalent fractions with the identified LCD.

- Students will solve problems that require them to add fractions with both common and unlike denominators.

- Students will convert an improper fraction to a mixed numeral.

After identifying the specific learning targets they will teach, teachers design their frequent formative assessments to gather data around these targets. They choose which learning targets need to be assessed and at what point in the unit. They don't need to assess every learning target but should choose those targets that they believe will have the most impact on student learning in the unit. Using the example of adding fractions, the teacher might design a short quiz with five to seven questions requiring students to find the least common denominator for a variety of fractions. The quiz will be given early in the unit, after students have learned this specific skill. The teacher will then decide what to do next for the students who didn't learn that target, as well as for the students who did. The formative assessments provide information about how to differentiate classroom instruction for the next lessons.

Select an Appropriate Assessment Format

Stiggins et al. (2004) describe four types of assessments: selected response, extended written response, performance, and personal communication. They suggest that once teachers have determined what type of learning target they are trying to assess, some methods of assessment will work better than others for that target. For example, selected-response questions can be used effectively to assess knowledge and reasoning targets but not performance or product targets. Performance assessments, on the other hand, can be used to assess all kinds of products, although they are likely to be too work-intensive to be used effectively to assess knowledge targets.

When determining what kind of assessment to use, teachers will want to consider how much time it takes to administer the assessment and how much time it takes to score it. Since the purpose of these assessments is to provide information to use immediately, the assessment must be scored and analyzed quickly.

Designing Quality Selected-Response Items

Once teachers have decided what type of assessment to write, it is important that they create an assessment that will produce data, or information, to help direct their teaching. Selected-response items (multiple-choice, true/false, matching, and fill-in-the-blank questions) have the advantage of being easy to score, especially with technology, and they can cover several different learning targets in one assessment (Stiggins et al., 2004). Carefully constructed items can ensure that teachers are getting the information they need to help them know what to do next.

Matching assessments are designed with two lists of words or phrases and ask students to match items from the left-hand list (premises) to items on the right-hand list (responses) (Popham, 2003). A good matching assessment will have more responses than premises so that students can't answer the ones they know and then guess at the remaining ones. There should also be homogeneous choices among the responses so that the context doesn't provide clues for students who really don't understand the information but can logically eliminate inappropriate choices (Stiggins et al., 2004).

True/false items require students to decide if the given statement is true or false. It is important that teachers make the statement either completely true or completely false so that statements that have some truth in them don't confuse students (Stiggins et al., 2004). Statements should be clearly written and should assess only one learning target at a time. Teachers should avoid using negatives, which might confuse some students who actually understand the material being assessed. The total number of items should be approximately balanced between true and false (Popham, 2003).

Multiple-choice items are typically composed of a sentence stem and a list of several options from which the students must choose the correct or best option as the answer. Teachers should remember that the intent is to see what the student knows about the learning target; therefore, they should take care to make sure the question itself isn't confusing or ambiguous. There are several ideas teachers will want to consider for writing good multiple-choice questions (Popham, 2003; Stiggins et al., 2004). The stem should contain a complete question and shouldn't have any negatives in it. For example, "Which of these is NOT one of the original colonies?" may be harder for students to answer because they might misinterpret the negative. If the stem is written as a question, the student sees the complete idea before trying to determine his or her response. Teachers should be cautious when using "all of the above" and "none of the above." They shouldn't give away the answer by giving options that wouldn't be grammatically correct, such as asking for something in the plural and having an option that is singular. Students can easily eliminate these options, which might allow them to guess the correct answer even if they don't understand the target being assessed.

Another point teachers will want to consider as they write multiple-choice items is how they will use the information from the completed assessment. Rebecca Kopriva (2008) suggests that teachers include carefully constructed wrong answers as options in multiple-choice questions and then use the resulting data to determine what it was that the students didn't understand. Did the question confuse them? Did they misunderstand the concept? When students choose options that were designed to reveal specifics about their thinking, teachers will know how to respond the next day. Teachers should keep in mind that the purpose is not to try to "trick" the student with the question, but rather to include those answers that will likely be chosen when a student has misunderstood the learning target.

For example, consider the following question:

What is the least common denominator for the following fractions?

$$\frac{1}{2} \qquad \frac{2}{3} \qquad \frac{3}{4}$$

    (a)   24

    (b)   12

    (c)   6

    (d)   9

The correct answer is, of course, (b) 12. However, the teacher included (a) 24 because students might multiply all three denominators together to get the answer, confusing the process to find greatest common factor with finding least common denominator. They also included (c) 6, thinking that students might multiply 2 and 3 and get 6 and figure that number is larger than the other denominator, 4.

Now, when the teacher goes back the next day to help students who need more instruction, she knows what students misunderstood during the initial instruction and can design her lesson plan accordingly.

Similarly, if teachers want to use selected-response items to assess more complex thinking, they must be thoughtful about how they write these items. Thomas Guskey and Jane Bailey (2001) cite an example of how to do this with a series of questions developed by Rutgers University professor Jeffrey Smith. The first question, a short-response item, asks who the seventeenth president was. Without any clues, students will probably consider this to be a hard question to answer, although many people know that Lincoln was the sixteenth president and that Andrew Johnson followed him. The same learning target could be assessed by using a multiple-choice question. If the options included Lincoln and Johnson, students might be able to answer the question more easily than they could without any clues. Consider, however, if the options were obviously wrong—for example, Clinton, Bush, and Washington—how easy the question would be. Thus, the rigor of the multiple-choice question can be increased or decreased by the options offered.

Designing Quality Extended-Response and Performance Assessments

When assessing a reasoning target, it is often easier for teachers to use an extended-response question if they want to really understand what students have learned or to know if they are able to pull together multiple pieces of information. While more difficult and time-consuming to score, extended-response questions allow teachers to more clearly understand students' learning needs and to provide more specific feedback.

When designing extended-response questions, a teacher should be careful to provide enough information in the question to ensure that students know what they are expected to do, so that the process of responding to the question doesn't get in the way of their demonstrating what they have learned. Stiggins et al. (2004) suggest, "To succeed with this assessment format, we must first write exercises that describe a single, complete, and novel task" (p. 174). They recommend giving students specific expectations for the answer, with enough context and support to make sure they understand the question. They suggest "pointing the way" (p. 175) with a reminder of the criteria the teacher expects the answer to meet, such as the number of details to be provided or the length of the response.

Both Popham (2003) and Stiggins et al. (2004) recommend *not* giving students choices of extended-response questions. When given choices, it's possible for students to pick a question on a topic that they know a great deal about and avoid a topic about which they're unclear.

Performance assessments ask students to complete a performance or create a product that demonstrates understanding of a process or the ability to perform a specific skill. For example, a music student might be asked to play a piece of music. Designing quality performance assessments involves establishing clear performance criteria and expectations. Students should know exactly what the criteria will be prior to the assessment.

Both extended-response items and performance assessments are generally scored using a rubric. If the teacher has determined the specific learning targets he or she wants to assess, these learning targets can easily be translated into the criteria that will be evaluated by the rubric (Arter & Chappuis, 2006). For example, if the student has been asked to design a scientific experiment with a *hypothesis,* a *control and variable,* and a *data-collection method* that will lead to an *appropriate conclusion,* those four items become the criteria for the rubric. Teachers can then provide specific levels or scores that define gradients of unacceptable/acceptable performance for each of these criteria.

Arranging Results for Successful Use

For teachers to be able to use the results of their formative assessment effectively, the results must be collected in a useful format. An item-analysis report of a multiple-choice test allows teachers to see not only how many students got each question correct, but also how many students chose each incorrect answer. Teachers can use this information to determine whether it makes sense to reteach a learning target to the whole group or only to those students who missed it. For example, if item analysis shows that only 5 percent of students chose the wrong answer for a particular multiple-choice question, the teacher will probably want to intervene only for those students who missed the correct answer. On the other hand, if 80 percent of students missed the answer, the teacher will likely reteach the concept to the whole class.

Teachers can also use item analysis to decide the best way to teach a group of students who need correctives. For example, if a multiple-choice item is designed so that each incorrect response represents a possible way the student might be confused, students who chose the same incorrect responses can be grouped together when the teacher provides intervention.

Similarly, teachers can use rubric data as a means to group students who need additional practice. For example, a writing rubric might score student work on three criteria: (1) use of transitions, (2) varying sentence length, and (3) word choice. Once the teacher scores the writing samples, the students can be grouped by areas of weakness for additional instruction and practice. For example, a group of students who scored low on the criterion for varying sentence length would receive help to address that specific skill.

The research is clear that frequent formative assessments make a difference for student learning (Black & Wiliam, 1998). It is important that teachers become confident users of the data they gather in the assessment process to make good decisions for their students. Creating a balanced assessment system that uses both formative and summative data will provide the information for teachers to set goals and make good instructional decisions. While designing quality assessments may be time-consuming, knowing what to do next for students is worth the time!

References

Ainsworth, L., & Viegut, D. (2006). *Common formative assessments: How to connect standards-based instruction and assessment.* Thousand Oaks, CA: Corwin.

Arter, J. A., & Chappuis, J. (2006). *Creating and recognizing quality rubrics.* Portland, OR: Educational Testing Service.

Black, P., & Wiliam, D. (1998). Inside the black box: Raising standards through classroom assessment. *Phi Delta Kappan, 86*(1), 8–21.

Christopher, S. (2007/2008). Homework: A few practice arrows. *Educational Leadership, 65*(4), 74–75.

Datnow, A., Park, V., & Kennedy, B. (2008). *Acting on data: How urban high schools use data to improve instruction.* Center on Educational Governance, University of Southern California, Rossier School of Education, Commissioned by NewSchools Venture Fund. Accessed at www.new. school.org/files/ActingonData.pdf on December 24, 2008.

Fisher, D., & Frey, N. (2007). *Checking for understanding: Formative assessment techniques for your classroom.* Alexandria, VA: Association for Supervision and Curriculum Development.

Guskey, T. R., & Bailey, J. M. (2001). *Developing grading and reporting systems for student learning.* Thousand Oaks, CA: Corwin.

Heritage, M. (2007). Formative assessment: What do teachers need to know and do? *Phi Delta Kappan, 89*(2). Accessed at www.kiva.net/~pdkintl/ kappan/k_v89/k0710her.htm on December 24, 2008.

Hoff, D. J. (2008, December). More schools facing sanctions under NCLB. *Education Week*. Accessed at www.edweek.org/ew/articles/ 2008/12/18/16/ayp.h28.html?tmp=559785571 on December 22, 2008.

Kopriva, R. (2008). What's wrong with wrong answers? *Harvard Education Letter, 24*(4), 6–8.

Leahy, S., Lyon, C., Thompson, M., & Wiliam, D. (2005). Classroom assessment: Minute by minute, day by day. *Educational Leadership, 63*(3). Accessed at www.ascd.org/publications/educational_leadership/nov05/ vol63/num03/Classroom_Assessment%40_Minute_by_Minute%2c_ Day_by_Day.aspx on October 27, 2007.

Marshall, K. (2008). Interim assessments: A user's guide. *Phi Delta Kappan*. Accessed at www.pdkintl.org/kappan/k_v90/k0809ma1.htm on October 5, 2008.

Mathematics content standards for CA public schools. (n.d.). Accessed at www.cde. ca.gov/be/st/ss/www.cde.ca.gov/be/st/ss on December 15, 2008.

O'Neill, J., & Conzemius, A. (2006). *The power of SMART goals: Using goals to improve student learning*. Bloomington, IN: Solution Tree.

Popham, W. J. (2003). *Test better, teach better: The instructional role of assessment*. Alexandria, VA: Association for Supervision and Curriculum Development.

Popham, W. J. (2008). *Transformative assessment*. Alexandria, VA: Association for Supervision and Curriculum Development.

Popham, W. J. (2008/2009). Anchoring down the data. *Educational Leadership, 66*(4), 85–86.

Schmoker, M. (1999). *Results: The key to continuous school improvement*. Alexandria, VA: Association for Supervision and Curriculum Development.

Stiggins, R. J., Arter, J. A., Chappuis, J., & Chappuis, S. (2004). *Classroom assessment for student learning: Doing it right—Using it well*. Portland, OR: ETS Assessment Training Institute.

WILLIAM M. FERRITER

 A National Board Certified Teacher, Bill Ferriter has been honored as a North Carolina Regional Teacher of the Year. Bill has worked as a contractor for Pearson Learning Solutions, designing professional development courses that empower educators with twenty-first-century skills. His trainings include the creative use of blogs, wikis, and podcasts in the classroom; the role of iTunes in teaching and learning; and the power of digital moviemaking for learning and expression. Bill has also developed schoolwide technology rubrics and surveys that identify student and staff digital proficiency at the building level. Bill has published articles in the *Journal of Staff Development, Educational Leadership,* and *Threshold.* Starting in September, 2009, he will write a column on technology in the classroom for *Educational Leadership.* His blog, the Tempered Radical, earned Best Teacher Blog of 2008 from Edublogs. He is a contributor to *The Principal as Assessment Leader* (2009) and the coauthor with Parry Graham of *Building a Professional Learning Community at Work*™ (Solution Tree, in press).

THREE

Yes, I Can: Responsible Assessment in an Era of Accountability

William M. Ferriter

No single aspect of teaching and learning has undergone greater changes—or come under greater scrutiny—in the recent past than the assessment of student learning. Our system is in the grips of a perceived crisis, failing in the eyes of policymakers and parents who are no longer satisfied with qualitative measures of accomplishment. Instead, education's stakeholders have begun to demand quantifiable results from everyone involved in schooling.

Consequently, the stakes are much higher for today's professional educators. Standardized tests—originally designed as simple tools for providing diagnostic information on the strengths and weaknesses of a community of students—are now considered valid indicators of the performance of everyone involved in the teaching-learning transaction (Koretz, 2008). Low student scores can result in failure for students, poor evaluations for teachers, and public ridicule and condemnation for schools.

The shift from testing for diagnosis to testing for accountability has served as a clarion call for schools and districts, changing the very nature of the work done with students. Decisions in classrooms are no longer a matter of simple judgment based on "professional opinions." Instead, teachers are urged to collect frequent data on the performance of their students. Courses throughout the curriculum are outlined methodically in pacing guides developed by "experts" who leave nothing to chance. Often teachers are hesitant to take advantage of teachable moments, fearing that they could leave classes falling behind (Perlstein, 2007).

In many ways, however, the new pressures introduced by accountability advocates have been long overdue. Without consequences, teachers gradually drifted away from delivering a guaranteed and viable curriculum, which educational researcher Robert Marzano (2003) identifies as the single greatest school-level variable influencing student achievement. Instead of systematically evaluating the time available for learning, determining objectives indispensable for all learners, and sequencing instruction in a logical way, schools left curricular decisions up to individual educators. Consistency across buildings was almost nonexistent.

Marzano goes on to argue that effective school leaders can immediately improve student achievement by ensuring that teachers across grade levels and content areas are intimately aware of—and focused on—the essential outcomes of their curricula:

> Ensuring that teachers address the essential content is necessary to implement a guaranteed and viable curriculum. . . . It is not uncommon for teachers to make idiosyncratic decisions regarding what to cover and what to leave out even within the context of highly structured curricula.

> To implement this criterion, administrators must monitor the coverage of the essential content. This does not necessarily mean that administrators have to "observe" the actual teaching of content. This would be so labor intensive as to be impossible. However, an administrator could ask teachers for evidence of adequate coverage in

the form of lesson plans, unit plans, or both. (Marzano, 2003, p. 31)

But holding teachers accountable for addressing the essential outcomes of their curricula—and for increasing rates of student achievement in their classrooms—can be nothing short of intimidating to practitioners unaccustomed to producing measurable results. Many resist, pointing to poor parenting, unsupportive principals, and insufficient professional development as the real reasons for the continuing struggles of their students (Muhammad, 2009). New expectations are seen as little more than unnecessary insults, feeding a sense of "anger and resentment among many educators and even more pessimism about the probability of making substantial and permanent change within schools" (Muhammad, 2009, p. 18).

Professional learning teams, on the other hand, are encouraged to embrace accountability as an opportunity to take ownership of student learning—the core product of education—and to see content mastery as their personal responsibility. The most accomplished learning teams are tackling these challenges by redesigning the way that they define their curriculum, engage students in their own learning, and systematically track progress in their classrooms.

This chapter is designed to show your team how to join the ranks of the empowered through responsible assessment.

An Assessment Nightmare

Standards became the cornerstone of most assessment programs in America with the reauthorization of the Elementary and Secondary Education Act—commonly known as No Child Left Behind—in 2001, which required states to maintain sets of identified standards for each grade level and content area and to frequently assess student proficiency in both reading and mathematics (Ainsworth, 2003).

For my team—a group of highly motivated sixth-grade social studies teachers in Apex, North Carolina—wrestling with standards began as we started to develop our first common assessments. Knowing that each assessment was supposed to be built on a set of essential outcomes collaboratively identified as appropriate for our students (DuFour, DuFour, Eaker, & Many, 2006), we printed the required curriculum for our subject area—a task that should not seem extraordinary. For us, however, it was the first time we had collectively examined the benchmarks defined by our state as essential for students to master. Over time, we had fallen into comfortable patterns, teaching content that motivated our students, fit into our personal interests, and/or aligned with the content taught by colleagues. Reflecting on standards together was something that we had never considered.

Our initial reaction was that we had made a horrible mistake! We were confronted by objectives that were difficult to understand, overly complex, or seemingly impossible to measure. While we were determined to accomplish our goal of creating a collection of common assessments based on a shared understanding of the content that we taught, we surrendered when we came across this knotty outcome in our state's social studies curriculum:

> **Objective 4.03:** The learner will examine key ethical ideas and values deriving from religious, artistic, political, economic, and educational traditions, as well as their diffusion over time, and assess their influence on the development of selected societies and regions in South America and Europe.

Without knowing it, we had stumbled onto a discovery already detailed by Robert Marzano (2006) in *Classroom Assessment and Grading That Work*: "National and state standards documents simply were not designed to allow for easy application to classroom assessments" (p. 18). Highlighting the philosophical underpinnings of subject areas and written in impenetrable terms by content-area specialists—groups described by Clayton Christensen, Curtis

Johnson, and Michael Horn (2008) as "intellectual cliques"—curriculum guides can leave teachers wondering what exactly their students are supposed to learn.

We grew increasingly frustrated when our school's leadership decided that we needed to post state objectives every day to inform students of the specific skills that each lesson would address. While we knew that student awareness of learning outcomes played a central role in successful classrooms, we argued passionately against this policy, believing that sixth-grade students would not understand language like *deriving from*, *diffusion over time*, and *assessing their influence on*.

Recognizing that process was far more important than product, our principal gave us an open invitation to create a system that would make our state's standards approachable to students and teachers alike, and then introduced us to the writing of Rick Stiggins, Robert Marzano, and Larry Ainsworth.

Deconstructing, Unwrapping, and Unpacking

We began by exploring *Classroom Assessment* for *Student Learning: Doing It Right—Using It Well* (2006) by Rick Stiggins, Judith Arter, Jan Chappuis, and Steve Chappuis. Determined to outline a student-driven, approachable model of classroom assessment that promotes—rather than simply assesses—learning, Stiggins and his colleagues believe that the key to effective assessment lies in clearly defining the measurable learning outcomes in state curriculum documents.

The challenge is that state benchmarks often include more than one measurable skill, requiring teachers interested in creating clear targets for learning to deconstruct their standards. Deconstructing standards involves "taking a broad and/or unclear standard, goal, or benchmark and breaking it into smaller, more explicit learning targets that can be incorporated into daily classroom teaching" (Stiggins et al., 2006, p. 80).

Deconstructing standards is a process recommended by nearly every national measurement and evaluation expert. Robert Marzano, for example, writes that teachers must "unpack the benchmarks in standards documents" and classify the individual "dimensions" measured by each objective (2006, pp. 17–18). For Larry Ainsworth (2003), identifying separate measurable elements in curricular objectives is called "unwrapping the standards." As he describes it, "Unwrapping the standards means to identify the concepts and skills found in both the standards (the *general* statements of learning outcomes—what students need to know and be able to do) and the indicators (the *grade-specific* learning outcomes)" (p. 5, emphasis in original).

Regardless of language, the central point remains the same: the complete scope of a curriculum only becomes clear when standards have been examined carefully for each of their component parts.

Once we recognized the importance of breaking standards into smaller measurable units—also called *unpacking*—my learning team decided to identify all of the individual skills that our state expected sixth-grade students to master. Because we had never been comfortable with the language of state standards, we were not sure where the unpacking process should begin. Eventually, we settled on a strategy suggested by Larry Ainsworth (2003):

> The next step is to carefully read through your selected standard and related indicators, and as you do so, **underline** the key concepts (important nouns and noun phrases) and **circle** the skills (the verbs). Remember, the concepts are what the students must know, and the skills or performance verbs are what they must be able to do. (p. 6)

Stiggins and his colleagues (2006) recommend a similar process, contending that state standards fall within four broad categories (or targets) of learning: knowledge, reasoning, skills, and products (see table 3.1).

Table 3.1: The Four Targets of Learning

Type of Target	Learning Outcomes*
Knowledge	Knowledge targets are fact-based learnings that can be easily assessed. For example: "The learner will identify historical events such as invasions, conquests, and migrations."
Reasoning	Reasoning targets require the application of knowledge to make comparisons, predictions, or evaluative judgments. For example: "The learner will evaluate the relationship between current issues and historical events such as invasions, conquests, and migrations."
Skills	Skills targets require an observable demonstration of the proper application of knowledge. For example: "The learner will manipulate information from tools such as maps, globes, charts, graphs, databases, and models to pose and answer questions about space and place, environment and society, and spatial dynamics and connections."
Products	Product targets require the application of knowledge to generate specific, predefined pieces of work common to a particular domain of study. For example: "The learner will create maps, charts, graphs, databases, and models as tools to illustrate information about different people, places, and regions in South America and Europe."

*Examples are from the North Carolina sixth-grade social studies curriculum.

Each type of learning target requires different skills and dispositions from students, dictating the type of instruction and evaluation necessary to ensure that an objective is properly addressed. Identifying the range of learning targets included in a curriculum is best done by spotlighting the types of verbs used in state standards and determining exactly what students are being asked to do (Stiggins et al., 2006).

Looking for specific action verbs in our curriculum served as a starting point for our learning team. Working with high-lighters, we were able to determine—in the course of a few hours—the complete range of knowledge, reasoning abilities, skills, and products that sixth-grade students were expected to master during the course of a school year.

What we discovered would not have surprised Marzano, Stiggins, or Ainsworth: our curriculum—which included thirteen competency goals and forty-three objectives—defined ninety different outcomes. Rather than standing alone as single expectations, each objective could be broken into at least two to four unique learning targets. Students were supposed to describe, evaluate, analyze, create, examine, identify, use, assess, trace, generate, manipulate, interpret, and compare topics connected to the government, economy, religion, environment, history, and cultural groups of both South America and Europe.

Think about the objective that first caused my colleagues frustration:

Objective 4.03: The learner will examine key ethical ideas and values deriving from religious, artistic, political, economic, and educational traditions, as well as their diffusion over time, and assess their influence on the development of selected societies and regions in South America and Europe.

In its simplest form, this objective required students to demonstrate mastery of three different abilities against two different backdrops (South America and Europe):

1. Examine ideas and values that have their foundations in the religious, artistic, political, economic, and educational traditions of countries and regions.

2. Explore how these ideas and values have spread through and between societies over time.

3. Assess the impact of these ideas and values on the development of societies.

However, a team attempting to completely and thoroughly analyze the standard can find multiple components within these three objectives. Table 3.2 shows the standard's startling complexity.

Table 3.2: One Deconstructed Objective

SOUTH AMERICA			EUROPE		
The student will . . .			The student will . . .		
Examine ideas and values drawn from:	Explore the spread of ideas and values drawn from:	Assess the impact of ideas and values drawn from:	Examine ideas and values drawn from:	Explore the spread of ideas and values drawn from:	Assess the impact of ideas and values drawn from:
• Religious traditions • Artistic traditions • Political traditions • Economic traditions • Educational traditions	• Religious traditions • Artistic traditions • Political traditions • Economic traditions • Educational traditions	• Religious traditions • Artistic traditions • Political traditions • Economic traditions • Educational traditions	• Religious traditions • Artistic traditions • Political traditions • Economic traditions • Educational traditions	• Religious traditions • Artistic traditions • Political traditions • Economic traditions • Educational traditions	• Religious traditions • Artistic traditions • Political traditions • Economic traditions • Educational traditions
in selected societies.	in selected societies.	on the development of selected societies.	in selected societies.	in selected societies.	on the development of selected societies.

Most shocking to us as we methodically worked our way through this process was that we had never even attempted to address many of our state's learning outcomes in our instruction. Like most sixth-grade social studies teachers, we overemphasized history in our classrooms. We engaged our students in studying the lives of the ancient Greeks and Romans in detail, dressing up in togas, making paper temples, and writing myths based on gods and goddesses.

Then we moved into an exploration of kings and castles, holding knighting ceremonies, writing illuminated manuscripts, and implementing grade-level codes of chivalry. We finished the year with fascinating units on the World Wars, holding seminars on the Holocaust and the role that nuclear weapons played in ending one of the greatest conflicts in history. Through it all, our students were highly motivated and engaged—and we were convinced that our instruction was top rate.

After examining our standards, though, we learned that our curriculum included only four history-based outcomes. Topics that consumed nearly 90 percent of our instructional time constituted less than 5 percent of the expectations set for sixth-grade students.

Deconstruction had forced us to confront a surprising and uncomfortable reality: the implemented curriculum in our classrooms was woefully incomplete when compared to the intended curriculum defined by our state. While we were accomplished educators recognized as school leaders, we had been making our instructional decisions without a systematic understanding of what was expected of our students.

Can We Really Teach Everything?

Embarrassed, our learning team resolved to begin carefully monitoring instructional decisions and aligning individual lessons to specific outcomes defined by our curriculum. To do so, we created a curriculum overview document (fig. 3.1) listing each of our original state standards alongside a collection of statements highlighting the range of outcomes required by each objective.

Objective 2.01: The learner will identify key physical characteristics such as landforms, water forms, and climate, and evaluate their influence on the development of cultures in selected South American and European regions.

Learning Targets

❑   The learner will identify key physical characteristics such as landforms, water forms, and climate in selected regions of South America and Europe.

❑   The learner will evaluate the influence that key physical characteristics such as landforms, water forms, and climate have on the development of cultures in selected regions of South America and Europe.

Figure 3.1: Structure of original curriculum overview document.

Our plan was to use this document much like a checklist, removing targets each time they were incorporated into our instruction. While this system would have been a simple way to ensure that required learnings were addressed in our instruction, it would not have made tracking performance by individual targets possible. Our initial document identified deconstructed standards separately, but each target remained grouped with its original objective.

Determined to better track student progress and coverage of the curriculum, we created a numbering system based on the structure of our original state standards document. Each learning target was assigned a unique four- or five-digit identifier that could be attached to assignments and assessment questions. Figure 3.2 (page 66) shows an example of this numbering system.

> **Objective 2.01**: The learner will identify key physical characteristics such as landforms, water forms, and climate, and evaluate their influence on the development of cultures in selected South American and European regions.
>
> **Learning Targets:**
>
> - **201.1**—The learner will identify key physical characteristics such as landforms, water forms, and climate in selected regions of South America and Europe.
>
> - **201.2**—The learner will evaluate the influence that key physical characteristics such as landforms, water forms, and climate have on the development of cultures in selected regions of South America and Europe.

Figure 3.2: Structure of revised curriculum overview document.

As we polished our curriculum overview document, we grew concerned about our ability to incorporate all of the measurable skills required by our curriculum into our classroom plans. As was the case in many states and districts, time for social studies had been drastically reduced in North Carolina as schools responded to the reading and mathematics testing requirements set by No Child Left Behind. With little more than forty-five minutes a day devoted to history, meeting ninety learning outcomes seemed unlikely at best.

Our worries were not unique. In fact, educators in nearly all content areas or grade levels are likely to find that the amount of material detailed in their state-adopted curriculum far exceeds the amount of available instructional time (Marzano, 2003). Unlike the narrowly focused expectations set for students in Europe and Asia, curricula in the United States emphasize quantity of coverage over depth of study (Schmidt, McKnight, & Raizen, 1996). Assessment expert Doug Reeves goes as far as to argue that state standards documents reflect a poor understanding of today's classroom:

The strength of one's belief in the standards fantasy is inversely proportional to the distance one is from the classroom. While many classroom teachers who face diverse learning needs and limited time know that rapid coverage of standards is not a substitute for student understanding, standards and curriculum designers at the district, state or national levels continue to publish documents that are distinguished more by their girth than their effectiveness. (Reeves, 2005, p. 48–49)

Responding to this reality, our team borrowed an idea from Marzano, who recommends that teachers and instructional experts at the district level identify and then eliminate nonessential outcomes in order to create a curriculum that can fit within the time available for instruction. Parent groups and neighborhood leaders can be enlisted to ensure alignment between community values and the benchmarks targeted for instruction (Marzano, 2006).

At first, this process seemed counterintuitive. After all, we had just finished articulating the complete scope and sequence of our curriculum. We were excited and determined to cover each deconstructed benchmark in our instruction. To intentionally ignore outcomes defined by state standards seemed unthinkable.

But we also understood that rushing through a curriculum was irresponsible—and experience had taught us that students mastered several objectives easily each year, either because they overlapped with the content covered in other classes or because they received unusual amounts of time and attention at other grade levels. Classroom assessment data and unit reflection documents offered a measure of assurance that labeling outcomes as "nonessential" did not mean we were shirking our responsibility to cover the curriculum. We knew that we could justify decisions to remove many learning targets from our instruction with simple pre-tests given early in a school year.

So we returned to our original list of ninety learning targets intent on identifying those that were critical for our students to master during the course of the school year. To center our decisions, our team began by generating a shared vision (fig. 3.3) of quality social studies instruction—something we had never done before—based on the foundational documents of the National Council for the Social Studies (1992).

Students of the twenty-first century will inherit a world that is increasingly interconnected. Natural and environmental challenges that cross boundaries will call for global solutions—and will be the source of primary conflict between nations. Networked governments and economies will also result in new opportunities for employers and employees. Those who can work across boundaries will be the most successful in this nontraditional tomorrow.

To be prepared for this future, our students must:

1. Understand the connections between natural resources and the success or failure of nations.

2. Recognize the impact that different forms of governments and economies have on standards of living.

3. Analyze the characteristics of culture that both link and separate different regions of the world.

4. Learn to manage information, draw conclusions, and take appropriate actions based on data.

Figure 3.3: Vision of quality social studies instruction.

To add structure to our curriculum review, we developed a checklist (table 3.3) to identify the learning targets defined in our state standards that supported our vision for quality social studies instruction. Each of our team members then worked through our learning targets, evaluating the alignment between individual outcomes, our shared vision, and our understanding of the strengths and weaknesses of our students.

Table 3.3: Alignment Checklist

Learning Target: _____	Yes	No
1. Does this learning target directly support our vision for social studies instruction?		
2. Does this learning target cover knowledge that will be new to our students and valuable to their continued study of today's world?		
3. Have our students demonstrated mastery of this learning target without direct instruction in previous years?		
4. Is this learning target addressed in other content areas or grade levels? If so, which ones?		
5. Would you recommend that we include this learning target on our list of essential outcomes for this school year?		

After each team member evaluated and identified the outcomes that were essential to meeting our vision for quality social studies instruction, we generated three lists: targets that received unanimous approval, targets that received unanimous rejection, and targets upon which our team had yet to come to consensus. Our initial review left us with thirty-one learning targets—out of an original ninety—that received support from our entire team and ten that needed further review.

During the course of a regularly scheduled meeting designed to discuss the ten remaining learning targets, we added six additional outcomes to our list of essential learnings, raising our total to thirty-seven. Overall, fifty-three targets defined by our state standards were labeled nonessential, and our curriculum had been narrowed by nearly 60 percent. As classroom teachers, we continued to struggle with the recognition that we were systematically eliminating elements from our required curriculum that could appear on state assessments in the future, but we also understood that each of us had been overlooking—or underteaching—other, more critical elements of the required curriculum. The care that we had put into identifying nonessential objectives based on a knowledge of our students and the curriculum in other grade levels and content areas gave us a measure of confidence in our final decisions.

Next, we assigned each identified outcome to a particular topic of study, and in the process discovered that countless lessons from existing units could be eliminated because they did not address essential learnings. By targeting our attention on only those deconstructed standards that aligned with our vision of quality social studies instruction, we had finally found time for the kinds of deep and meaningful learning experiences that had all but been eliminated from our classrooms as we rushed through an unwieldy curriculum.

Our work finally had the kind of clarity and focus necessary to create new systems for responsible assessment!

Making Learning Approachable With Unit Overview Sheets and "I Can" Statements

While our learning team made great progress at understanding our state standards and creating a more manageable curriculum based on essential outcomes, we still were not satisfied with our final product because our deconstructed standards remained unapproachable, loaded with language that would easily confuse twelve-year-old students. For example:

201.2: The learner will evaluate the influence that key physical characteristics such as landforms, water forms, and climate have on the development of cultures in selected regions of South America and Europe.

202.3: The learner will evaluate the impact of changing distribution patterns in population, resources, and climate on the environment in South America and Europe.

401.3: The learner will evaluate the impact of migration on the political, economic, and social development of South America and Europe.

501.2: The learner will assess the impact of the location of natural resources on the economic development of selected regions, cultures, and countries of South America and Europe.

602.1: The learner will analyze the influence of education and technology on productivity and economic development in selected countries and regions of South America and Europe.

1003.2: The learner will compare the rights and responsibilities of citizens in selected contemporary societies in South America and Europe to each other and to the United States.

Phrases like these seemed no more instructionally valuable than our original standards. Rick Stiggins and his colleagues (2006) agree, explaining that classroom learning targets must be written in student-friendly language to be of any value:

> Students cannot assess their own learning or set goals to work toward without a clear vision of the intended learning. When they do try to assess their own achievement without understanding the learning targets they have been working toward, their conclusions are vague and unhelpful. . . . Making targets clear to students at the outset of learning is the fundamental underpinning to any assessment for learning practices we will implement. (p. 59)

For our learning team, the emphasis on objectives written in student-friendly language carried great resonance because our work with deconstructing standards started with a challenge from our principal to design a system to engage students in their own learning.

Writing learning targets in student-friendly language is not a complicated or intimidating process. It simply involves beginning each target with an approachable phrase like "I can" or "I am learning to," defining uncommon words in an age-appropriate way, and including an action that can be observed or measured

(Stiggins et al., 2006). With little effort, our team converted our deconstructed standards into "I Can" statements (table 3.4) and developed overview sheets highlighting the essential learnings and content knowledge that we intended to address in our units of instruction (fig. 3.4).

Table 3.4: Sample "I Can" Statements

Original Learning Target	Student-Friendly "I Can" Statement
202.3: The learner will evaluate the impact of changing distribution patterns in population, resources, and climate on the environment in South America and Europe.	202.3: I can judge how changes in population, resources, and climate effect the environment of South America and Europe. This means that I can make predictions and draw conclusions about what might happen to the environment in places where populations rise, resources fall, or the climate changes.
501.2: The learner will assess the impact of the location of natural resources on the economic development of selected regions, cultures, and countries of South America and Europe.	501.2: I can determine how the location of natural resources has changed the economies of different countries in South America and Europe. This means that I can decide which natural resources have made countries stronger and which natural resources have made countries weaker, and that I can list the most important natural resources in the world today.
1003.2: The learner will compare the rights and responsibilities of citizens in selected contemporary societies in South America and Europe to each other and to the United States.	1003.2: I can compare the rights and responsibilities of citizens in the United States to the rights and responsibilities of citizens in several different South American and European countries. This means that I can list similarities and differences between the kinds of opportunities that people have in countries around the world.

Unit: Southern Europe

Over the next two weeks, we'll be studying the countries of Southern Europe. One of the greatest challenges facing Southern Europe is dealing with thousands of African immigrants who arrive illegally each year. Managing these immigrants is placing a huge financial burden on countries like Spain, Italy, and Malta. What's more, new immigrants are bringing new cultures and customs that are not always understood or valued.

We will study the reasons that Africans are choosing to move to Southern Europe and the impact that this movement is having on life for the Italians, Spanish, and Maltese. We will also explore possible solutions to this challenge, ranging from stricter controls over immigrants to support programs for African nations.

Learning Target	Task 1	Task 2	Task 3
203.1: I can examine the different reasons that people move to and from countries. This means that I can inspect data related to movement and correctly identify the main causes for migration.			

Rate your own mastery of this learning target. Remember that your rating can change over time:

New to Me ————————————————————➤ **I Got This!**

401.3: I can judge the impact that migration has on governments, economies, and cultures. This means that I can make predictions and draw conclusions about what might happen to the governments, economies, and cultures in countries that are struggling with immigrants.			

Rate your own mastery of this learning target. Remember that your rating can change over time:

New to Me ————————————————————➤ **I Got This!**

501.1: I can determine how the location of natural resources has an impact on economies. This means that I can look at different kinds of natural resources and decide which will help countries to grow stronger and which will leave countries weak.			

Rate your own mastery of this learning target. Remember that your rating can change over time:

New to Me ————————————————————➤ **I Got This!**

Figure 3.4: Sample unit overview sheet.

Unit overview sheets now play an integral role in our efforts to engage students in their own learning. As we begin a unit of study, students review new essential learnings, finding connections to earlier content and selecting outcomes as the focus for independent projects. Each lesson is directly connected to individual learning targets, allowing students to track progress by recording the results of classroom assignments. The process provides regular opportunities for self-assessment, and students revisit evaluations as they demonstrate new understandings over time.

The importance of bringing transparency to the expected outcomes of instruction is undeniable. Students in classrooms where learning targets are clear feel a sense of ownership and empowerment that increases motivation and personal satisfaction (Stiggins et al., 2006). Learning targets also create frameworks for finding patterns between seemingly unrelated topics. Organizing information becomes easier in classrooms where connections are constantly made to small sets of essential learnings revisited over time (Ainsworth, 2003).

Finally, establishing clear goals for student learning has a measurable impact on student achievement (Marzano, 2003). Classrooms where students understand the learning outcomes for daily lessons see performance rates 20 percent higher than those where learning outcomes are unclear. Student-friendly statements of deconstructed standards also provide an objective measure against which learners can compare their own performance. Such concrete, immediate, ongoing feedback on the mastery of specific skills has an equally powerful influence on student success (Marzano, 2003).

On our team, each unit overview sheet contains no more than five learning targets for students to master. While we often indirectly address additional learning targets during the course of a unit of instruction, we intentionally focus primary attention on a handful of key objectives. Our goal is to make self-assessment of learning manageable for students—an unlikely outcome when the number of measurement topics per unit becomes cumbersome or overwhelming (Marzano, 2006).

We also realized that our unit overview sheets were equally valuable as effective vehicles for communication between home and school—another school-level factor linked to improved student achievement (Marzano, 2003). Parents—who are often as intimidated by state standards as students—can provide more targeted and specific academic support to their children when they are presented with lists of learning targets written in language that they can understand (Stiggins et al., 2006).

Breaking down complex standards into approachable learning elements has made understanding the outcomes for our class logical. When the targets are paired with clear tasks that can be used to demonstrate learning, parents can determine which targets need more attention and be creative in extending learning at home. No longer is there confusion about whether students have mastered classroom content. Instead, parents can independently draw accurate conclusions regarding the successes and struggles of their children.

Driven by or Drowning in Data?

For perhaps the first time in our teaching careers, our team had crafted a shared definition of exactly what we wanted our students to know and be able to do. We understood the standards set for students by our state curriculum and had articulated a collective vision for quality social studies instruction. We identified a manageable collection of essential learnings that could be consistently implemented in every social studies classroom and created a system for engaging students and parents as partners in learning. We were *finally* ready to create common assessments!

While deconstructing the standards for our course had taken a significant amount of time, it was a critical step that teams often incorrectly skip. Breaking a curriculum into student-friendly learning targets lends much-needed focus to instructional decisions and makes measuring and monitoring practical and possible. Teams with a collection of discrete learning targets can create systems where data are collected and manipulated by outcome, allowing for trouble-free regrouping of students as well as targeted planning for the future. Common assessments built from a detailed picture of exactly what students are to learn are far more effective than assessments built without a shared understanding of the curriculum (Stiggins et al., 2006).

Clarifying essential outcomes also allows teams to redesign systems of reporting student performance. No longer are parents and students limited to general grades for entire content areas or units of study. Instead, feedback can be shared at the individual skill level, highlighting student strengths and weaknesses *within* discrete performance categories (Marzano, 2003). Assessments that provide such fine-grained feedback help learners to "avoid damaging generalizations" about overall ability in a subject area based on limited understandings of mastery (Stiggins et al., 2006, p. 61).

Our learning team's effort to build assessments began by generating sets of questions aligned directly with the specific outcomes covered in particular units. All members of our team reviewed every question and labeled it with the numerical identifier of the learning target it was designed to measure (fig. 3.5).

Next, the team developed simple test tracking sheets to make disaggregation of student performance data possible. (See table 3.5, page 79.) As they graded assessments, teachers recorded incorrect student responses to individual questions. Visually, these tracking sheets made content mastery by student and class easy to judge. Rows with high numbers of marks identified students who were struggling with our curriculum, and columns with high numbers of marks identified concepts that needed reteaching.

Learning Outcome: Comparing African and Southern European Nations

Country	GDP per Capita	Literacy Rate	Life Expectancy
Italy	$25,100	99%	80
Greece	$19,100	98%	78
Spain	$21,200	98%	79
Nigeria	$900	68%	52
Mali	$900	51%	43
Senegal	$1,500	40%	53

Question: Based on this table, which of the following statements about migration from Africa to Southern Europe are likely to be true? (Check all that apply.) (*Learning Target 203.1*)

❑   People move from Africa to Southern Europe because they can get better medical care.

❑   People move from Africa to Southern Europe because the governments of Southern Europe are welcoming and inviting.

❑   People move from Africa to Southern Europe because the climate is more appealing.

❑   People move from Africa to Southern Europe because they have the potential to earn more money.

❑   People move from Africa to Southern Europe because they can get a better education.

Question: Immigration has recently become a major issue in the United States. Politicians regularly speak about their plans for dealing with waves of people that move to America from Central and South America. Based on our study of Southern Europe, should we be worried about immigration? What kind of impact could large numbers of new residents have on our country? (*Learning Target 401.3*)

continued on next page →

Figure 3.5: Sample assessment questions aligned with specific learning targets.

Question: In recent years, there has been great interest in identifying crops that can be converted into biofuels to run cars. One such crop is Jatropha, a hardy plant that is resistant to drought and produces seeds that are up to 40% oil. Many companies are beginning to plant Jatropha in Africa, where land is readily available for low prices. What impact could this new plant have on African countries? (Check all that apply.) *(Learning Target 501.1)*

- ❑   Residents will be forced off of their land, increasing migration to Southern Europe.

- ❑   Governments will prevent Jatropha from being grown in Africa because of its environmental dangers.

- ❑   New jobs will be created on Jatropha farms, increasing the quality of life in Africa and decreasing migration to Southern Europe.

- ❑   Migrants who left Africa for a better life will return home to their countries as the economy steadily improves.

- ❑   Southern Europeans will begin immigrating to Africa, looking to improve the quality of their lives.

As we began to disaggregate data by target, we struggled with a temptation to gather huge quantities of information before drawing conclusions about student learning. We wrote long assessments with dozens of questions connected to each outcome—and we buckled under the weight of the data that we had collected. Frustrated with the amount of time spent simply recording results and our inability to see patterns in the pages of information that we had collected, we questioned our decision to track performance at the question level.

Our mistake is not uncommon among those who rely on information to make critical decisions. In his 2005 book *Blink: The Power of Thinking Without Thinking*, bestselling author Malcolm Gladwell explains that volume can lend a sense of false confidence to those looking for solutions to challenging problems. Quality thinking ends up compromised by unnecessary

Table 3.5: Sample Test Tracking Sheets

Southern Europe Assessment			
Student Name	Question 1: Target 203.1	Question 2: Target 401.3	Question 3: Target 501.1
Student 1	X		X
Student 2			
Student 3			
Student 4			
Student 5		X	
Student 6	X		
Student 7	X		
Student 8			
Student 9			
Student 10	X		
Student 11	X		X
Student 12			
Student 13			
Student 14	X	X	X
Student 15	X		
Student 16	X		
Student 17	X		
x = Incorrect student response			

data. Good decision makers, by contrast, identify a handful of key indicators for each situation and see unrelated information as a distraction. Gladwell calls this process *editing:*

> The second lesson is that in good decision making, frugality matters. . . . To be a successful decision maker, we have to edit. . . . I think we get in trouble when this process of editing is disrupted—when we can't edit, or we don't know what to edit, or our environment doesn't let us edit . . . If you are forced to consider much more than your unconscious is comfortable with, you get paralyzed. (2005, Kindle location 2040–2060)

Realizing that our data-management patterns were leaving us paralyzed, our team revisited each of the common assessments that we had written, identifying the questions that we believed best measured student understanding of our deconstructed standards. Questions with overly complex language were revised to ensure that vocabulary did not interfere with a student's ability to demonstrate mastery. Questions with tasks that did not align properly with the outcomes defined by our learning targets were corrected. While this process was contentious at times, it resulted in highly polished questions in which we had great confidence.

For each learning target, we selected two assessment questions to serve as the primary indicators of student mastery. While we would not ignore student responses to other questions—or overlook student performance on classroom assignments connected to individual learning targets—our data collection, decision making, and direction setting would be centered on these primary indicators. We then identified exemplars of—and rubrics for—high-quality responses to all open-ended questions, standardizing grading across classrooms and providing students with comparisons to consider while reflecting on their own learning. (See the sample in fig. 3.6.)

Ironically, our decision to edit the information we collected when making decisions about student learning had benefits beyond the workroom. Managing less information made it possible to offer parents and students feedback that was far more targeted. No longer were we drowning in numbers, struggling to identify the individual skills that students had yet to master. Instead, we began offering detailed explanations for what students had learned—and how we knew they had learned it.

Learning Target 401.3: I can judge the impact that migration has on governments, economies, and cultures. This means that I can make predictions and draw conclusions about what might happen to the governments, economies, and cultures in countries that are struggling with immigrants.

Primary Indicator: Immigration has recently become a major issue in the United States. Politicians regularly speak about their plans for dealing with waves of people that move to America from Central and South America. Based on our study of Southern Europe, should we be worried about immigration? What kind of impact could large numbers of new residents have on our country? *(Learning Target 401.3)*

Exemplar	Strengths of Response
The United States should be concerned about immigration because the cost of supporting new residents can be overwhelming. As populations increase, governments must find ways to pay for more public services such as schools, roads, and police officers. Another concern is that troubles can often break out between new residents and existing citizens because they don't understand each other. This can cause tensions and sometimes violence. While immigrants often improve a country over time, there are definitely bumps in the road to be ready for.	1. Student starts with a clear statement of position. 2. Student specifically addresses the economic challenges of migration—providing additional public services for an increased population. 3. Student recognizes that responding to these challenges is a responsibility of government. 4. Student identifies cultural misunderstandings that result when new immigrant groups come to a country.

Figure 3.6: Exemplar for open-ended assessment question.

Lessons Learned

Responding to new expectations in an era of accountability, schools and districts are exerting greater control over the work of classroom teachers than ever before. Feedback on the mastery of learning is expected to be focused and specific—and educators, once given the professional courtesy to set direction for instruction without question or consequence, must carefully align their work with state standards in order to produce results on end-of-grade exams.

At times, teachers balk at these changes. We question the consequences of a single-minded focus on standardized testing and wonder what we have lost by attempting to numerically define the knowledge, skills, and abilities of the students in our classrooms. Passion for learning, we contend, has been replaced by pressure to perform.

What we rarely question, however, is our obligation to students. This commitment to kids is probably best articulated by Mike Schmoker in a 2004 article for the *School Administrator*:

> For all of the current controversy surrounding issues of student achievement and accountability, we forget that there is far less controversy about our shared desire to help more children learn, to reduce the achievement gap, and to improve the quality of the complex work of teaching in all schools, from urban to rural, from economically struggling to affluent. (p. 48)

For the empowered team, fulfilling this desire to help more children learn begins with a shared understanding of the kinds of knowledge and skills defined by state curricula. Finally, it requires designing assessments that effectively measure the skills that we expect students to learn—and developing new systems for identifying and reporting what our students know.

While this process may initially sound intimidating, five simple steps can make it approachable to every learning team:

1. **Carefully deconstruct your state standards.** For better or for worse, state standards are rarely written in language that can be understood or assessed without difficulty. Each standard must be broken down into its component parts (multiple measurable skills) before the complete scope of a curriculum can be realized.

Highlighting action verbs is a quick first step for identifying the individual outcomes that students are expected to master (Ainsworth, 2003; Stiggins et al., 2006). Teams may also want to develop a numbering system for identifying specific deconstructed learning targets. Doing so makes it possible to collect, manage, and report data by individual outcome.

2. **Identify essential—and eliminate nonessential— outcomes.** In one of his most controversial findings, Robert Marzano (2003) has shown that the time required to address the complete scope of most state curricula far exceeds the amount of time actually available for instruction, forcing teachers to make a somewhat counterintuitive decision: selecting learning targets to address and ignore during the course of a year's instruction. This process can be formalized when teams create shared visions for effective instruction in their content area and use alignment checklists to review learning outcomes defined by deconstructed standards.

3. **Write learning targets in student-friendly language.** Engaging students in assessing their own learning can have a profound impact on achievement at any school. Making self-monitoring possible begins by converting deconstructed standards into student-friendly statements of learning that can be posted on a daily basis and attached to assignments and assessments. Student-friendly statements of learning often begin with approachable phrases such as "I can" or "I will be able to." They also define unfamiliar vocabulary words and end with tasks that can be demonstrated or measured (Stiggins et al., 2006). Teachers who rewrite benchmarks in approachable language for their students enlist and empower unexpected allies in their efforts to drive academic change.

4. **Create unit overview sheets.** Teams interested in bringing additional clarity to their work also develop overview sheets that define the skills addressed in individual units of teaching. The most effective unit overview sheets include a description of the content to be studied, a handful of student-friendly learning targets to be addressed, a place for tracking performance, and a method for students to record personal learning reflections. In many ways, unit overview sheets serve as curriculum maps—ensuring that teams are addressing essential outcomes—and as promising vehicles for jargon-free communication with parents and students.

5. **Avoid drowning in data.** Deconstructed standards, student-friendly learning targets, and unit overview sheets make powerful assessments possible as teachers tie individual questions to—and report to parents on—mastery of discrete skills. Simple tracking forms quickly indicate gaps in learning and allow regrouping for enrichment and remediation. The risk of such fine-grained approaches to assessment is that teams and teachers will drown in unnecessary volumes of student learning data. Primary indicators—small collections of preselected questions that indicate content mastery—as well as exemplars of accomplished responses and shared scoring rubrics can ensure that data management is doable.

Richard DuFour, Robert Eaker, and Rebecca DuFour passionately believe that the potential to drive change in public education rests within our hands. "At no time in our history," they write, "have we, as a profession, possessed a clearer sense of what it takes to help all students learn at high levels. The question remains: will we demonstrate the discipline and tenacity to act on that knowledge?" (2005, p. 252)

What is most powerful about the ideas of Rick Stiggins, Robert Marzano, and Larry Ainsworth outlined in this chapter is that they are practical steps toward improving schools that lie directly within the sphere of influence of every tenacious teacher. Today, teams can sit down and deconstruct standards. Today, teams can identify essential outcomes and write student-friendly learning targets. Today, teams can generate unit overview sheets, create opportunities for students to reflect on their learning, and develop assessments that give feedback on the mastery of discrete skills.

Today, teams can redesign assessment to help more students learn at higher levels. All that is required is a bit of determination and a commitment to work systematically in the face of professional challenge.

Does your team have the discipline to make that change?

References

Ainsworth, L. (2003). *"Unwrapping" the standards: A simple process to make standards manageable.* Englewood, CO: Lead & Learn.

Christensen, C. M., Johnson, C. W., & Horn, M. B. (2008). *Disrupting class: How disruptive innovation will change the way the world learns.* New York: McGraw-Hill.

DuFour, R., DuFour, R., Eaker, R., & Many, T. (2006). *Learning by doing: A handbook for professional learning communities at work.* Bloomington, IN: Solution Tree.

DuFour, R., Eaker, R., & DuFour, R. (Eds.). (2005). *On common ground: The power of professional learning communities.* Bloomington, IN: Solution Tree (formerly National Educational Service).

Gladwell, M. (2005). *Blink: The power of thinking without thinking.* New York: Back Bay Books.

Koretz, D. (2008). *Measuring up: What educational testing really tells us.* Cambridge, MA: Harvard University.

Marzano, R. J. (2003). *What works in schools: Translating research into action.* Alexandria, VA: Association for Supervision and Curriculum Development.

Marzano, R. J. (2006). *Classroom assessment and grading that work.* Alexandria, VA: Association for Supervision and Curriculum Development.

Muhammad, A. (2009). *Transforming school culture: How to overcome staff division*. Bloomington, IN: Solution Tree.

National Council for the Social Studies. (1992). *A vision of powerful teaching and learning in the social studies: Building social understanding and civic efficacy*. Accessed at www.socialstudies.org/positions/powerful on August 31, 2008.

Perlstein, L. (2007). *Tested: One American school struggles to make the grade*. New York: Henry Holt and Company.

Reeves, D. (2005). Putting it all together: Standards, assessment, and accountability in successful professional learning communities. In R. DuFour, R. Eaker, & R. DuFour (Eds.), *On common ground: The power of professional learning communities* (pp. 45–63). Bloomington, IN: Solution Tree (formerly National Educational Service).

Schmoker, M. (2004). Here and now: Improving teaching and learning. *School Administrator, 61*(10), 48–49.

Schmidt, W. H., McKnight, C. C., & Raizen, S. A. (1996). *Splintered vision: An investigation of U.S. science and mathematics education: Executive summary*. Lansing, MI: U.S. National Research Center for the Third International Mathematics and Science Study, Michigan State University.

Stiggins, R., Arter, J., Chappuis, J., & Chappuis, S. (2006). *Classroom assessment* for *student learning: Doing it right—Using it well*. Upper Saddle River, NJ: Pearson Education.

PART TWO

Collecting, Interpreting, and Reporting Data

MICHELLE GOODWIN

Michelle Goodwin, a twenty-two-year veteran of education, is associate super-intendent for Instruction for Montcalm Area and Ionia County Intermediate School Districts in Michigan. In this capacity, she serves the needs of over a thousand teachers, administrators, and paraprofessionals by securing or directly providing professional development in the areas of assessment, preK–12 Eng-lish language arts, and K–3 literacy/ Reading First. She assists with new teacher training, school improvement, and data analysis. In addition, Michelle serves as the county coordinator for state assessments. Her collaborative work includes participation in and leadership of the Consortium of Mid-Michigan Instruction Teams and state-level assessment projects. As a high-school classroom teacher, Michelle taught English language arts to students at risk and with special needs, most often within a co-teaching arrangement.

FOUR

Matchmaker, Matchmaker, Write Me a Test

Michelle Goodwin

Most educators realize there is more to creating good assessments than meets the eye. As teachers, we do our best to explain assignments to students, but sometimes we receive a product we did not expect or even consider as a possibility; we create tests or quizzes we think measure exactly what we taught, only to see half the class does poorly on them. Experience reinforces that there is not only an art to creating good assessments, but also a science. But before we assume that educators must deeply understand statistics and be able to talk about the "p value" of assessment items in order to create respectable classroom assessments, let me offer this reassurance: when teachers and students are clear about the learning targets that must be met and will be assessed, and when teachers create assessment items or tasks that are carefully matched to these targets, then, more often than not, we get back data that we can use to change our instruction to best meet student needs. For student involvement in this work, "if assessments are to support improvements in student learning, their results must inform students how to do better next time" (Phi Delta Kappa International, 2006, p. 1).

Educator and author Laurence J. Peter (n. d.) once chided, "If you don't know where you are going, you will probably end up somewhere else." Getting into the practice of creating quality assessments, whether they will be used formatively or summatively, is like this—if we do not have a clear sense of the learning target we want students to hit, and if we are not careful to ensure we have the best method for assessing that target, we are likely to end up with results we were not expecting. But when we take care to match the intended learning targets with the best methods for assessing student understanding or competency on those targets, we and our students will be rewarded with specific information that is useful for helping each student take the next step in the learning progression toward mastery of the standard.

Embedded in a linear process, the steps for ensuring proper alignment of learning target with type of assessment would simply look like this: (1) "unpack" or otherwise "deconstruct" a standard into clear learning targets, (2) identify the specific type of each learning target, (3) link each target to the best type of assessment for eliciting information on student learning, and (4) use the created items in an assessment and review whether or not the assessment reflected student learning or lack thereof.

Beginning With Clear Targets

A *standard* answers the question, where am I going in my learning? while *learning targets* show students the path to get there (see Popham, 2008, on progressions). Learning targets are those specific statements, typically written in language friendly to students (and therefore parents), that tell what a student needs to know and/or be able to do on the way to meeting a standard or benchmark. Think in terms of progression. If, as a student, I am able to do one step, and then the next and the next after that, the likelihood that I am able to meet the standard is greatly increased. Both the teacher and the student monitor student progress on this path and make adjustments to the teaching and the learning along the way. Depending on the standard, the content targets or "stepping stones" to reach the standard may or may not have to be sequenced in a specific order.

Let's consider a specific example that illustrates clear learning targets. The state of Pennsylvania, through what it calls *assessment anchors* and *eligible content*, has partially delineated learning targets for teachers. What remains is for teachers to rephrase the eligible content (that is, the intended learning) into student-friendly language. Whether a teacher follows the six steps for unpacking standards as outlined by Rick Stiggins, Judith Arter, Jan Chappuis, and Steve Chappuis (2004) or the four steps for creating learning progressions as defined by James Popham (2008), the idea is to arrive at clear statements that show teachers and students how the standard will translate into student work. Whether we call this process for making standards accessible *unpacking* (Stiggins et al., 2004), *unwrapping* (Ainsworth, 2003), *identifying subskills and enabling knowledge* (Popham, 2008), or any other term such as *deconstructing*, its result must identify what students need to know and do *on the way* to mastering a given standard. While state curriculum or standards documents may suggest that "standards" indicate what students need to know or be able to do, often those standards are written too broadly to be easily useable—hence the need to "unpack" them. Table 4.1 shows a partial learning progression from Pennsylvania's sixth-grade reading standards.

Table 4.1: Sixth-Grade Reading Standards

Standard 1.1 Learning to Read Independently	Assessment Anchor R6.A.1—Understand fiction appropriate to grade level. R6.A.1.2—Identify and apply word recognition skills.	Eligible Content R6.A.1.2.1—Identify how the meaning of a word is changed when an affix is added; identify the meaning of a word from the text with an affix.
Standard 1.2 Read Critically in All Content Areas		

Source: Pennsylvania Department of Education, 2006

Stiggins et al. (2004) suggest that learning targets such as these be phrased in student-friendly language. Thus, a teacher might present his or her students with the learning targets shown in table 4.2 (page 92).

Table 4.2: Sixth-Grade Reading Standards in Student-Friendly Language

Standard 1.1 Learning to Read Independently	Assessment Anchor R6.A.1—Understand fiction appropriate to grade level. R6.A.1.2—Identify and apply word recognition skills.	Eligible Content R6.A.1.2.1—Identify how the meaning of a word is changed when an affix is added; identify the meaning of a word from the text with an affix.	Student-Friendly Targets I can give the definition of an affix. I can pick out the affix in a word; I can pick out the prefix or suffix in a word. I can tell what the affix means. I can tell what new meaning a word has when the affix is added.
Standard 1.2 Read Critically in All Content Areas			

When studying this example, some teachers will remark that taking the skill statement and breaking it into such specific targets seems time-consuming. After all, most teachers, or at least English teachers, would know they will have to define *affix* for students. However, completing the deconstructing process forces teachers to be intentional and ensures that students are not left to guess the steps to mastery. Once the students know what an affix is, where to find it, and its meaning, they can apply that knowledge to figure out what a word means or how the meaning of a word has changed. Thus, the students meet the standard and take ownership of their learning.

Figure 4.1 shows an example of a science standard from Michigan put into student-friendly language using this process.

Types of Targets

When state standards are deconstructed, the learning targets tend to fall into one of four categories that typically build upon one another: knowledge targets, reasoning targets, performance skills, and product targets (Stiggins et al., 2006). Any given standard will have one or more types of these targets within it.

GLCE P.FM.05.31: Describe what happens when two forces act on an object in the same or opposing directions.

Learning Target(s):

- I can give the definition of *force*.

- I can tell what 3 changes might happen to an object when a force is applied.

- I can write in words and also create a diagram to explain what happens when two forces act on an object in the same direction.

- I can write in words and create a diagram to explain what happens when two forces act on an object in opposite directions.

Sources: Michigan Department of Education, 2007 (content expectations) and Julie Milewski, Ionia Public Schools, Ionia, Michigan, 2008 (learning targets; used with permission)

Figure 4.1: Content expectations for fifth-grade science with learning targets.

Knowledge Targets

Knowledge targets measure what facts and concepts a student knows. "I can find the verb in a sentence" or "I can list three major systems of the body" are knowledge targets, as is "I can explain the important characteristics of U.S. citizenship." Knowledge targets can also include procedural knowledge (knowing how to do or use something): "I can draw a circle using a compass and label the radius and diameter." Many knowledge targets are easy to identify and create from a standard. They should not be ignored or dismissed and are an important base for the other types of targets.

Reasoning Targets

Reasoning targets focus on the use or application of knowledge. When seeking to identify reasoning targets, look for verbs within standards such as *analyze, predict, conclude,* and *evaluate.* For example, in art class, a student may know the characteristics of oil paints (knowledge target) and then use that information to choose or evaluate the appropriate type of canvas and brush in order to create specific artistic effects. In physical education, after learning facts about aerobic versus anaerobic exercise, a student may be able to analyze a fitness routine to decide if it is beneficial to her or not.

Skill or Performance Targets

Those targets that must actually be demonstrated and observed to be assessed are called skill or performance targets. With skill targets, a student combines knowledge and reasoning to act. The process of execution is the important aspect, regardless of what the process produces. "I can use a microscope correctly" is an example of a skill target. To meet the target, the student would know the parts of a microscope, reason out which objective lens to use based on what is needed to be seen, and be able to adjust the coarse and fine focus without cracking the cover slip or slide. Using a writing process is also a good example of a skill target, especially as we need to distinguish performance from the next type of target: products.

Product Targets

In the English language arts or literacy classroom, students are taught that writing is a process. The first stage is prewriting, followed by drafting, revising, editing, and then publishing. However these stages are defined, in the end, whether the student has gone through a five-step or a six-step process, the result is a product such as a written essay. Having taught language arts for many years, I know that there are as many ways as there are students to get to that product. As a teacher, I had to be very careful about what I actually assessed. If I needed to assess a student's use of a writing process or any particular strategy in the process, I had to observe it. Just because a student completed and turned in a product was no guarantee that she used the process I was trying to teach. The product—in this example, an essay—stands on its own and should be assessed as a product.

Table 4.3 shows a possible learning progression for a standard from Michigan's high school English language arts content expectations.

Table 4.3: A Learning Progression for a Grade 9 English Language Arts Standard

Standard 1.1—Understand and practice writing as a recursive process.	
Content Expectation 1.1.4—Compose drafts that convey an impression, express an opinion, raise a question, argue a position, explore a topic, tell a story, or serve another purpose, while simultaneously considering the constraints and possibilities (e.g., structure, language, use of conventions of grammar, usage, and mechanics) of the selected form or genre.	**Unpacked for English 9**—Write paragraphs that present a dominant impression (descriptive), give an opinion and support it (persuasive), tell a story (narrative), or explore and explain a topic (expository). Be sure to use appropriate grammar, sentence length and structure, and word choice/specialized vocabulary for each type of writing.
Learning Targets	
1. _____ I can develop an opinion on a given topic, write that opinion clearly as a complete sentence (not a question), and start my paragraphs with this sentence.	
2. _____ I can find at least 3 different and valid reasons to support this opinion.	
3. _____ I can write these reasons out clearly, using vocabulary appropriate to the topic and to my reader and having a new sentence for each new reason.	
4. _____ I can put these reasons in my paragraph in an easy-to-follow, logical order with transitions.	
5. _____ I can see the opposition's viewpoint and acknowledge it in my writing.	
6. _____ I can indent the first line of my paragraph.	
7. _____ I can write complete sentences, making sure I include some that are short, some medium, and some longer.	

Source: Deborah Clark, Portland High School, Portland, Michigan, 2008. Used with permission.

In this example, the teacher has chosen for students to complete a persuasive essay. The learning targets are structured to allow students to use them as a checklist or analytic rubric to gauge their progress while writing or revising. The product, the final essay, will be summatively assessed for a grade. The process of writing is observed and assessed formatively, as the learning targets are met, but in a product target, what ultimately matters is the quality of the product itself. The grade or score comes from assessing the product summatively against a scoring guide such as an analytic or holistic rubric.

Understanding Methods of Assessment

With the creation of clear learning targets, the first half of the match is in order. To begin filling in the second half of the equation, teachers must understand the methods of assessment that are available, the strengths and weaknesses of each method, and how a particular method fits with the type of learning target. There are typically three acknowledged types of assessment methods: selected response, constructed or extended written response, and performance. Stiggins et al. (2004) also include personal communication, as does Ken O'Connor (2002). Each method has its benefits and drawbacks, depending on what type of learning target you are assessing.

Selected Response

Most teachers are familiar with and commonly use selected response as their main form of assessment. Selected-response items include multiple choice (probably the most used type of question [Linn & Miller, 2005]), matching, dichotomous choice—otherwise known as true/false or any other either/or choice (Fisher & Frey, 2007)—fill in the blank, and labeling a diagram. (Note: Fill-in-the-blank and diagram-labeling items are sometimes considered constructed-response items. Such short tasks are included here as selected-response items because they require typically one or two word answers.) These methods may be used in formative or summative manners, using paper and pencil, hand signals, or the like.

One of the benefits of using selected response is that items are easy to score or mark. Additionally, when written well, these items, particularly multiple-choice items, can be used not only for assessing basic knowledge but also for analyzing incorrect responses and assessing students' levels of understanding or reasoning skills. Table 4.4 (page 98) shows how a teacher can create a multiple-choice item that will serve these functions. First, the teacher writes the *stem*—the question part of the item: "How is a plant able to grow larger?" Then, the teacher comes up with the possible answers a student might choose. In addition to the *key*, or correct answer (D), the teacher writes plausible but incorrect answers (called *distractors*), each of which is designed to alert the teacher to a particular category of error in student thinking. In this example, choice A represents a misconception; choice B, an oversimplification; and choice C, an overgeneralization. The third column in table 4.4 shows the teacher's more specific interpretations of student answers. If any students select A, the teacher then knows to address student understanding of the role of soil versus sunlight in the process of photosynthesis and the fact that a plant produces food internally. Carefully formatted in this way, multiple-choice items can be a quick and efficient method for assessing several dimensions of student learning.

A teacher needs to create distractors in a careful manner so as to get information that will be valuable for the next steps in student learning or to reveal what reteaching or extensions to learning are needed. Typically, it is sufficient for a multiple-choice item to have three distractors. For lower elementary grades and students with reading difficulties, two distractors may be suitable. Using two distractors keeps the item simple enough to help avoid frustration for those students who are still learning to read or for those who struggle with too much text.

Table 4.4: Distractors in a Selected-Response Assessment Item

How is a plant able to grow larger?		
A. It gets its food from the soil.	Misconception	Does not understand that nutrients are made internally by the plant.
B. It turns water and air into sugar.	Oversimplification	Understands that food is made internally but does not understand that water and CO2 are used to make sugar and O2.
C. It has chlorophyll to produce food.	Overgeneralization	Does not understand that some parasitic plants do not contain chlorophyll.
D. It adds biomass through photosynthesis.	Correct answer	

Source: From *Checking for Understanding: Formative Assessment Techniques for Your Classroom* (p. 108), by Douglas Fisher and Nancy Frey, Alexandria, VA: ASCD. © 2007 ASCD. Used with permission. Learn more about ASCD at www.ascd.org.

Constructed Response

Constructed response requires students to gather their knowledge or understandings about a topic, organize their thoughts, and then present them in written form. Constructed responses can be short, such as a few sentences answering a science question, explaining a math process, or defining a social studies concept. They can also be extended written responses such as essays. Although relatively time-consuming to score, constructed-response items can elicit information about student knowledge and reasoning skills and are not necessarily as difficult to create as good selected-response items. Consider this example:

> In strip mining, layers of soil and rock are removed in order to expose minerals. Name three effects of strip mining on land. Explain how each of these might affect communities nearby.

Asking students to only name three effects of strip mining keeps this item at the knowledge level. Notice how the item is written to draw out first what knowledge a student has about strip mining and then what reasoning the student can apply to that knowledge.

Performance

Music rehearsals and concerts, speeches, and physical activities are all examples of performances, as would be the *use* of any product. Creating a functional electrical circuit in science class has a performance aspect not only in the constructing of the circuit, but also in using it to flow current through the wires and turn on a light bulb. When the process a student must undertake is the important aspect of a standard, when actions must be observed in order to be assessed, or if the process is integral to the creation of a product, then using performance as the method of assessment is very suitable. For example, the learning target "I can use correct form to shoot an accurate free throw" must be observed on several levels. At the knowledge level, a student must know where to find the free throw line on the court. The teacher must see the student use a technically sound body position to set the basketball. The amount of force used to throw or push the ball toward the net must be observed. Without this direct observation, if the ball does not reach the net or go through the net, the teacher and the student are not likely to be able to know where in the process an error or problem occurred. Unclear wording of the task or target may interfere in how the student actually performs the task. If the target read, "I can shoot a free throw," there would not necessarily be a focus on form, which could affect accuracy. Again, as with any type of item, the teacher must be very clear when creating the target and connected items; otherwise, the performance a student gives may yield something else altogether.

When creating tasks for students to perform, it is wise to make sure that the performance can be completed in a safe environment. Here we are talking about concern not only for students' physical safety (an obvious example would be making sure that the gymnasium floor is not wet at the free throw line if a student is shooting baskets), but also for their emotional safety. We all know someone, for example, who dislikes speaking in front of others. In a classroom that stresses risk taking and emphasizes participation without the fear of undue criticism, or in a classroom where a student knows the teacher will not tolerate taunting or bullying, a student is likely to give a performance that is a more accurate representation of his or her knowledge and skills than if the environment is not seen as safe.

Another consideration in using performance assessments is time. While I may be able to observe a student's knowledge and reasoning skills through a performance, I may not always have the time to do so. Instead, a selected-response item might illicit proper and accurate information needed on the student's learning. Let's consider an example from mathematics: symmetry. When teaching students about symmetry, I could explain and demonstrate by drawing on the board each of the four forms of symmetry: rotation, reflection, transformation, and glide reflection. I could have students practice understanding these forms using manipulatives while I rove around the classroom and formatively assess whether or not students understand these concepts by watching how they actually turn, flip, or otherwise move the manipulatives and into what positions. In a formative manner, this performance on students' parts would allow me to ask them questions, further clarify misunderstandings with them, and provide any other necessary feedback. However, as a summative assessment, this observation would be time consuming. I could just as easily provide students with a handout showing diagrams of the types of symmetry and have students label the different forms. Or I could have students create their own examples by drawing figures that represent the four types of symmetry. I would still be assessing student knowledge and reasoning, just through a more expeditious format. Thus, performance assessment tasks are not necessarily appropriate for knowledge or reasoning learning targets, depending on the content, time, and other factors.

Personal Communication

Examples of using personal communication as a method of assessment include but are not limited to oral questioning or examination, learning logs and journals, conferring, and presentations (Stiggins et al., 2004; O'Connor, 2002). Again, it is important for the teacher to word the task clearly and to create a safe, comfortable learning atmosphere. As with performances, a student who is not comfortable in the classroom in front of others is less likely to provide the teacher with the best example of his or her learning during the personal communication experience.

Time is also a consideration with personal communication tasks, and variable depending on the learning target. A musical performance usually takes a specific amount of time, for example. In a learning log or journal, used as personal communication, however, one student might explain something well enough in one paragraph while another student takes two or three paragraphs. Depending on the learning target, length may or may not matter.

Time issues can be mitigated to some extent via a well-written learning target. Many educators remember "oral comps" from our undergraduate or graduate work. We had a specific amount of time set by our professors during which we had to defend, explain, or otherwise talk about a certain topic. We knew that time limit ahead of time and prepared ourselves accordingly. Likewise, in the use of learning logs or journals during class, a teacher can manage the time necessary for student responses and her own scoring time by telling students that their response should be a certain number of sentences or paragraphs.

Another factor to consider is how personal communication, such as asking questions to an entire class, may create problems for assessing other learners. As Douglas Fisher and Nancy Frey (2007) point out, "When one student is provided the opportunity to answer, the ability to check for understanding with the larger group is lost" (p. 22). If I ask one student to name the parts of a kayak out loud and other students hear the response, correctly given or not, my assessment is no longer valid for other individuals. I have lost any ability to discern whether or not students knew the answer on their own or were simply repeating what they had heard. There are ways around this, such as the use of small whiteboards; the teacher poses a question, and each student writes an answer on his or her board. When asked to show their answers, the students hold up their marker boards for the teacher to see. At a glance around the room, the teacher sees who has answered in what ways—whose answers are plainly incorrect or inadequate—and can instantly decide to address the issues with the whole class or provide another question and touch base with those having difficulties. (See Fisher & Frey [2007] for additional suggestions for using oral communication as a method of assessment.)

Making the Match

Now that we have a basic foundation in creating clear learning targets and understanding the methods of assessment, we are ready for *target-method match* (Stiggins et al., 2004). If we are indeed to create assessments or individual assessment items that meet the needs of students to monitor their own learning and take the next steps, and if we are to make appropriate decisions about our own teaching and what we need to do next to assist students, then we must consciously and with great intention choose the assessment methods that best match the learning targets and standards. If there is not harmony between the target to be assessed and the method chosen to assess it, we will get information that is not useful and results that may be misleading. Without a proper match, we thwart our ability to see patterns in student thought and learning. Charts like table 4.5 provide an accessible resource that teachers can keep close at hand while playing matchmaker.

Table 4.5: Aligning Learning Targets to Assessment Methods

Type of Target to Be Assessed	Assessment Method			
	Selected Response	Constructed Response/ Essay	Performance Assessment	Personal Communication
Knowledge	Good match	Good match	Not a good match	Partial match
Reasoning	Partial match	Good match	Good match	Good match
Performance Skills	Not a good match	Not a good match	Good match	Partial match
Product	Not a good match	Partial match	Good match	Not a good match

Source: From *Classroom Assessment* for *Student Learning* (p. 100), by R. Stiggins, J. Arter, J. Chappuis, and S. Chappuis. Copyright 2006 ETS/Assessment Training Institute. Used with permission.

Matching Knowledge Targets to Assessment Methods

Knowledge targets are perhaps the easiest to match to an assessment method. Selected-response items, especially in terms of the efficiency and simplicity of overall scoring, can measure student recall of facts, procedures, definitions, and the like most easily. Teachers are familiar with selected-response items since they are found on most, if not all, state tests and in textbook materials, including software test-item banks. Selected-response items make it possible for a teacher to observe at a glance patterns within groups of students. For example, if approximately equal numbers of students chose each answer A, B, C, and D, then it appears that the students who answered incorrectly guessed the answer. This assumes that the items are well constructed and intended to reveal misconceptions and misunderstandings in student reasoning and thinking (Fisher & Frey, 2007). When such results are quickly available, changes to instruction can follow shortly thereafter.

Knowledge targets can also be assessed through constructed-response items. For example, instead of simply labeling a picture of a microscope, students can list the parts and write about what each part is for and how it functions. Students could be asked to describe how to prepare and use a slide, thereby showing an understanding of how the microscope parts work together. Identifying the functions of a microscope is still a knowledge target, but in this instance, more information about student thinking can be culled from a constructed response than from a selected-response format.

Performance assessments are not a good match with knowledge targets. We might be tempted to assume that if a student can do something, he or she must have the knowledge behind it. However, after someone shows me how to drive a car, I can do so without knowing all the parts of the car or all the rules of the road. I might be able to hit a free throw without knowing anything about the game of basketball. Most likely I would not do either of these things well, but being able to perform a task may or may not mean I know what I need to know.

Personal communication, on the other hand, provides a partial match for knowledge targets. The teacher can ask follow-up questions of the student or ask the student to elaborate his or her response. Using personal communication for knowledge targets can be a time-consuming option. If students are responding in learning logs, for example, the teacher must decide if he or she will read all the logs every time or will sample student answers. The teacher's actions will be based on whether the personal communication is being used formatively or summatively. If the logs are being formatively used, a sample of student responses may be adequate; if used summatively, all the logs will need to be read and scored by the teacher. Either way, students must know what aspects of the communication will count toward the score. In a science learning log, how important is spelling and punctuation? In math, how important is it to show the steps in solving a problem? Again, the learning target will determine the need for explicitness in a student's answer.

Matching Reasoning Targets to Assessment Methods

Reasoning targets are best assessed with constructed-response, performance, or personal communication assessment methods. Teachers can use a selected-response format for assessing reasoning targets, but doing so requires careful construction of the items, especially if they are intended to reveal the levels and perhaps basic patterns of student reasoning. This is why reasoning targets are only a partial match with the selected-response method.

A better match for reasoning targets is the constructed response. In writing, a student can take time to explain his or her thinking. Essay-response items in particular can elicit a great deal of reasoning and thinking skills. Time—the teacher's as well as the student's—is a consideration when using extended constructed-response methods such as the essay. While it is relatively easy to write questions for this type of assessment, the teacher will spend more time on the other end of the process in reading student responses.

Performance assessments also match relatively well with reasoning targets. As a student is performing a task, the teacher can observe as one action leads to another. The focus here is on how a student applies knowledge. As a student, I may know how to turn the steering wheel of a car to make the wheels turn in one direction or another. Through application of this knowledge, I learn or reason that I cannot turn the wheel quickly enough on a turn to straighten the wheels. I reason that I need to let the wheel slip through my hands as the turn is completed. If I make the turn but do not release the wheel, the car potentially ends up on the curb. In gym class, I know how to properly stand and swing a bat to hit a baseball. I take one hit, and the ball goes a few feet in front of me; I take a bigger or harder swing, and the ball soars. Over time, I learn to adjust my swing to meet the need to send the ball closer or farther, to the left or more to the right. I could explain to someone how to do this (through an essay or personal communication), but when the teacher sees both performances and notes the change, my reasoning as a student is evident.

Personal communication also works well as a method to assess reasoning skills. With oral communication, we can gauge students' thinking by engaging them in conversation and asking follow-up questions. As mentioned earlier, we must be aware that once one student answers a question aloud, the validity of the answers other students might give may be skewed by what has already been heard.

Matching Skill or Performance Targets to Assessment Methods

By definition, the best way to evaluate a student's proficiency on a skill is to have the student perform the skill. While a student can explain through personal communication how to do something or can choose the steps of a process in the correct order on a selected-response assessment, we must actually observe skill targets in action to judge student proficiency. We can assess the knowledge pieces that lead to a performance—"I know how to hold the flute correctly"—but holding the flute correctly does not guarantee that the student can play it. Going back to the microscope example, just because a student can identify the parts of a microscope (knowledge target) and reason that the smaller a sample is, the greater the magnification needed (reasoning target), we must watch a student put those two targets together to appropriately adjust the focus so as to get a clear picture without cracking the cover slip. Likewise, if I am evaluating the process a student uses to create a term paper, I must collect evidence that a student used a graphic organizer, I must observe two students conferring, and I must watch the student taking notes on 3 x 5 cards. A student can tell me (personal communication) that he or she took them, and I can collect evidence of that, but if I am truly evaluating the process of writing a term paper, I must observe all of the steps in the process.

Matching Product Targets to Assessment Methods

For a product target, the best assessment match is a performance. The caution here is that we as teachers must make sure we have defined for students exactly what it is that we are assessing, since observing students as they create the product is not always necessary. As a teacher, I can read an essay or a paper a student completes without having had the benefit of seeing the prewriting, drafting, and so on. In other words, I can assess a student's paper *as a product* that meets or does not meet a product target without needing to know how it was created. (Contrast this to the situation described in the previous section, in which the performance target of carrying out the writing process was the focus of the assessment.) How I assess the paper as a teacher and what I assess it for must be determined *before* I give the assignment or assessment task to students and certainly before I mark it formatively or grade it summatively.

Selected-response assessment does not match well with product targets. Constructed-response assessment is a partial match for a product target: a student can write out the steps for baking a cake, for example, and the teacher can be reasonably assured that when the directions are followed, the cake will be edible. However, if I really want to know if a student can make a cake, I need to see and most likely taste the cake. When evaluating the attributes of a product is necessary for determining a student's proficiency in creating that product, we must actually have the product. No multiple-choice question and no amount of student ability in describing through personal communication how to complete a product can adequately address the actual quality of the product.

Implications for Practice

Teachers are being increasingly required to make data-based decisions, but a focus on data alone is not sufficient to create the changes in instruction that we need to see. It is imperative that teachers learn to create assessments—whether formative or summative—that meet their needs and, more importantly, the needs of their students. Creating quality assessments and individual assessment items is not something to be left to testing companies or textbook-related item banks. Teachers need real-time data for real-time decisions. Knowing how to identify clear targets is integral to knowing what to teach and in what sequence. This knowledge must be combined with an understanding of what types of assessments are available and best suited to particular targets. If we are to become truly in tune with the learning our students need, we cannot leave the matching of target to method to someone else—even if that someone is the trusted town matchmaker. This is our role as teachers, and we must embrace it.

References

Ainsworth, L. (2003). *"Unwrapping" the standards: A simple process to make standards manageable.* Denver: Advanced Learning.

Fisher, D., & Frey, N. (2007). *Checking for understanding: Formative assessment techniques for your classroom.* Alexandria, VA: Association for Supervision and Curriculum Development.

Linn, R. L., & Miller, M. D. (2005). *Measurement and assessment in teaching* (9th ed.). Upper Saddle River, NJ: Merrill, Prentice Hall.

Michigan Department of Education. (2007). *Science grade level content expectations.* Accessed at www.michigan.gov/documents/mde/Complete_Science_GLCE_12–12–07_218314_7.pdf on December 15, 2008.

O'Connor, K. (2002). *How to grade for learning: Linking grades to standards.* Thousand Oaks, CA: Corwin.

Pennsylvania Department of Education. (2006). *Reading assessment anchors.* Accessed at www.pde.state.pa.us/a_and_t/lib/a_and_t/Reading_Assessment_Anchors_intro.pdf on December 15, 2008.

Peter, L. J. (n.d.) Accessed at www.quotationspage.com/quote/353.html on February 9, 2009.

Phi Delta Kappa International. (2006, November/December). Executive summary. *EDge, 2*(2), 1.

Popham, W. J. (2008). *Transformative assessment.* Alexandria, VA: Association for Supervision and Curriculum Development.

Stiggins, R. J., Arter, J. A., Chappuis, J., & Chappuis, S. (2004). *Assessment for learning: An action guide for school leaders.* Portland, OR: ETS Assessment Training Institute.

Stiggins, R. J., Arter, J., Chappuis, J., & Chappuis, S. (2006). *Classroom assessment for student learning: Doing it right—Using it well.* Portland, OR: Educational Testing Service.

TAMMY HEFLEBOWER

 As director of curriculum, instruction, and interim assessment for Douglas County Public Schools near Denver, Colorado, Dr. Tammy Heflebower ensures that every student in every classroom receives a quality education. Dr. Heflebower is a seasoned practitioner and public speaker with experience at the classroom and administrative levels. She earned her doctorate of education in educational administration from the University of Nebraska-Lincoln, and completed the Cooperative Urban Teacher Education Program in Kansas City, Missouri. As a fourth-grade teacher in Columbus, Nebraska, she received the District Distinguished Elementary Teacher Award. Dr. Heflebower has also worked as a middle school administrator; director of professional development; National Educational Trainer for the National Resource and Training Center at Girls and Boys Town in Nebraska; and adjunct professor of curriculum, instruction, and assessment courses at several universities. A prominent member of numerous educational organizations, Dr. Heflebower has served as president of the Nebraska Association for Supervision and Curriculum Development and as legislative liaison and board member for the Colorado Association of Educational Specialists. Her articles have been featured in the monthly newsletter *Nebraska Council of School Administrators Today* and other publications. She is a contributor to *The Principal as Assessment Leader* (Solution Tree, 2009).

FIVE

Proficiency: More Than a Grade

Tammy Heflebower

As teachers, we often complain that students don't care about learning, only the scores they receive. Yet many of us unknowingly perpetuate this attitude by our own practices. Monitoring student progress is a daunting task in and of itself, even without taking into account inconsistencies within our grading procedures. We know a great deal about our content and our students. When we engage in collegial efforts and professional dialogue regarding student proficiencies, we obtain more coherence and consistency in our evaluation and communication systems as well. As Anthony Alvarado notes, "Isolation is the enemy of improvement" (quoted in Wagner, 2008, p. 157). Collaborating as grade-level teams offers a great structure to engage in these conversations, yet structure is not enough. Teachers need relevant, timely, trustworthy information about student performance results. This chapter will discuss how to understand and respond to those results through creating proficiency level descriptions, developing a range of quality assessment items aligned to proficiency levels, setting mastery cut scores, and improving grading practices.

Clearly understanding the complexities of student achievement makes our daily instructional and programmatic decisions more meaningful and accurate. Once we create descriptions for each level of competence, our conversations can center on proficiency rather than the grade, mark, or score. Additionally, enhancing our abilities to write and understand quality assessments allows us to see how they vary in complexity and difficulty. Knowing that proficiency levels and the corresponding assessments vary, we then realize that student achievement cannot best be measured by a single arbitrary grading scale. The time has come to stop arguing about one one-hundredth of a percentage point and to concentrate on the learning instead.

Creating Proficiency Level Descriptions

One way to begin the new conversation about learning is to engage with one another in the creation of proficiency level descriptions (PLDs) for the essential learnings or standards we are teaching. Some districts and authors may call these essential learnings *benchmarks, standards, big ideas,* or *anchors.* These PLDs require us to determine the knowledge, skills, and dispositions that characterize any given essential learning or standard. To some teachers, this will resemble rubric writing. It is similar, yet not identical. PLDs are used to identify knowledge and skills for broader learning concepts, while rubrics tend to be more specific to a lesson or unit objective, specifying the finite variances among narrower topics and objectives. Well-written assessments use PLDs as the foundation for item writing. Many PLDs are included in the technical manuals that accompany state and norm-referenced assessments and may be called by different names such as *achievement level definitions.* Teachers using textbook assessments as the basis of their evaluations may have to request PLDs from the textbook company. Figure 5.1 is an example of the definitions established for levels of performance on a state achievement test.

Proficiency level descriptions allow us to identify not only differences between proficient and nonproficient work, but also the degree of proficiency on a continuum. In other words, is a student at the beginning level or very close to the proficiency cut? A proficiency *cut score* is that fine line that separates students who demonstrate the knowledge and skills deemed necessary for proficiency in an essential learning or standard and those who do not yet demonstrate such knowledge and skills.

Advanced (4)	A student scoring at the Advanced Level has success with the most challenging content of the Colorado Model Content Standards. These students answer most of the test questions correctly, including the most challenging questions.
Proficient (3)	A student scoring at the Proficient Level has success with the challenging content of the Colorado Model Content Standards. These students answer most of the test questions correctly, but may have only some success with questions that reflect the most challenging content.
Partially Proficient (2)	A student scoring at the Partially Proficient Level has limited success with the challenging content of the Colorado Model Content Standards. These students may demonstrate inconsistent performance, answer many of the test questions correctly, but are generally less successful with questions that are most challenging.
Unsatisfactory (1)	A student scoring at the Unsatisfactory Level has little success with the challenging content of the Colorado Model Content Standards.

Source: Colorado Department of Education, 2008

Figure 5.1: Achievement level definitions.

By clearly noting what it takes for students to truly master a concept or skill, we can better respond to student needs with various interventions. Too often, we only move students into varied grade-level content rather than deeper thinking, further application, and/or problem-solving within the existing grade-level content.

To develop PLDs, assemble a team that includes new and veteran teachers familiar with the content and the grade level of students being assessed; knowing how "typical" students perform within the specified content area is helpful in creating accurate descriptions. Examine national and state content standards for the grade level, and refer to Larry Ainsworth's considerations for "power standards." These include: "(1) *endurance* (Will this provide knowledge and skills that will be of value beyond a single test date? . . .), (2) *leverage* (Will this provide knowledge and skills that will be of value in multiple disciplines?), and (3) *readiness* for the next level of learning (Will this provide students with the tools they need for success at the next level or grade?)" (Ainsworth, 2003, p. 13)

Define Proficiency Levels and Their Characteristics

Next, a team leader facilitates a discussion about the characteristics of student performance at each of four levels: *beginning, progressing, proficient*, and *advanced*. (Your team might choose to align your terminology with district or state progressions.) It is not imperative to have four levels, but that number is recommended to help the team better understand students' varying abilities and depth of understanding. In primary grades, two levels (proficient and nonproficient) may be sufficient, as student skill levels may not vary as much for certain skill sets. Usually, however, using four levels allows the assessor to take a stand on student work as either more proficient (proficient and advanced) or less proficient (beginning or progressing). When there are five categories, teachers may be tempted to make determinations in the middle of the scale (to award a three on a five-point scale), and three categories may not allow enough specificity regarding the student's degree of proficiency. These four levels are also closely connected to the four levels for Title I NCLB requirements, and most states and districts also use four levels of proficiency.

Each of the four general levels can be broken into its own continuum of knowledge, skills, and abilities. For example, the low end of the proficient category might be *barely proficient*, which means that a student has demonstrated the minimum competencies to be classified within that category. A student obtaining a more thorough understanding or application of the knowledge and skills listed within that same category would be at the *upper proficient* level. The same is true for each respective category, *barely beginning* and *upper beginning, barely progressing* and *upper progressing, barely advanced* and *upper advanced*. Clearly identifying the knowledge and skills for each categorization allows you to note how a student achieves within the levels. A *barely progressing* student likely needs different interventions than a student closer to the cut score for proficiency. The *barely advanced* student simply meets the minimum of the advanced category, whereas a student in the *upper advanced* category demonstrates a deeper knowledge and application of the characteristics of the advanced category. There is a continuum of abilities even within the same classification category. Figure 5.2 is a useful visual for organizing the conversation.

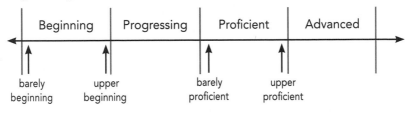

Figure 5.2: A continuum of proficiency levels.

Most teams tend to discuss the proficient category first, starting by describing the characteristics of barely proficient performance. The team leader lists the characteristics and posts them in front of the group. Then the team moves on to the discussion and recording of the characteristics of barely progressing and barely advanced performance. Knowledge and skills that do not reach the barely progressing level default to the beginning category.

Refine Characteristics of Performance

The team continues to discuss the differences between each level and revises the descriptions. The team leader might use figure 5.2 to facilitate this process by marking various locations along the spectrum and asking, "What is the difference between the student performance at the *barely beginning* level and that at the *upper progressing* level?" The group might then discuss how both students would be classified as nonproficient, yet the student demonstrating knowledge and abilities at the *barely beginning* level is at a much lower performance level. They then work together to clearly articulate the knowledge and skills that separate, if even slightly, each level.

The leader could follow that discussion by asking, "What interventions might we use with the student at the upper progressing category (just to the left of the proficiency cut?) How are they different from those used for students at the beginning level?" The varying proficiency degrees correlate to the kinds of interventions teachers might use. Teachers would use more intensive intervention strategies with the beginning student than we might for the upper progressing student. The team members will often come up with responses such as, "Students just below the cut might only need one more example or a clarification of a commonly made error in thinking or processing. The students at the *barely beginning* to *beginning* level might need more direct instruction in multiple learning styles—auditory, visual, kinesthetic, for example—visual examples, or maybe manipulatives to assist in better understanding." Through this process of discussing and revising, the entire team reaches consensus on the proficiency level descriptions, how to identify them, and how to adjust instruction in response.

Adjust Descriptions Based on Actual Performance

It is important to note that empirical evidence (actual student results) may create the need to revisit the drafted proficiency level descriptions occasionally (Nebraska Department of Education, 2007). Sometimes we under- or overestimate proficiency for certain essential learnings or standards; we may predict specific writing skills for proficiency, for example, but student results over time may indicate that such expectations are unrealistic for typical writers at that grade level. Looking at actual student performances over time serves as a reality check.

Developing Assessment Items

We can use these proficiency level descriptions to create assessment items within a teacher-created assessment tool, and we can also use them to be good "consumers" of assessments readily available through a textbook or other resource. After we have collaboratively created our own or deciphered the textbook proficiency level descriptions, we use those PLDs to assist us in identifying the types of items we have on our assessments. Do we have questions that represent each of the varied proficiency levels on the assessments we are using? A student achieving at the *barely beginning* level of proficiency will need different, and often more intensive, interventions than a student falling toward the *upper progressing* level. Such data are the foundation for our differentiation strategies.

Providing varied levels (beginning through advanced items) on classroom-based assessments helps ensure opportunities for students of differing abilities to demonstrate their knowledge more accurately. For example, including *a couple* of beginning-level assessment items or tasks might seem too easy, yet for a struggling student, this provides an opportunity to get some assessment items correct, and more clearly shows the difference between what he or she knows and has yet to understand. The same is true at the upper end; including *several* advanced items (not just proficient-level items) allows an advanced learner to demonstrate more of his or her understanding. I recall a kindergarten teacher using a checklist to explain to a parent that the student had mastered counting numbers one through ten. When the parent asked where the student stopped, the teacher said, "Well, I don't know. I didn't ask him to count beyond ten." Both the teacher and the parent know some information, yet one might argue that a kindergartner who knows the counting patterns beyond 10—say, to 21, 31, 101, and 1001—knows more about counting patterns than a student who stops at ten. Therefore, by not providing more advanced opportunities on this oral assessment, the teacher may not have collected solid information to determine the best instruction for that child.

Provide Multiple Opportunities

Most teachers will find that the items on any given assessment fall mostly into the proficient or progressing categories. This certainly gives us some information about whether a student is proficient or not on the essential knowledge or skill sets. However, creating assessment opportunities for all proficiency levels allows us to ascertain which *degree* of proficiency or nonproficiency students can attain. There is no magic number of items to include at each level of proficiency; simply ensure that multiple opportunities exist for students to demonstrate those varied levels. Examine the number, types, and quality of items. One selected-response item such as a true/false question at the beginning level, for example, is not sufficient to determine that level of understanding, since a student might guess the correct answer. Teachers must include a sufficient number of well-written items in order to have confidence that student performance accurately reflects student knowledge. Including more items at the progressing and proficient levels may be desirable, as the cut score between proficient and nonproficient is the most critical.

After comparing your assessment items to your PLDs, revise to include a range of item types and proficiency levels within your assessment. To assist in adding levels of difficulty, you may want to use a taxonomy such as Bloom's (Bloom & Krathwohl, 1956) or Marzano's (Marzano & Kendall, 2007), or a protocol for levels of thinking (Ritchhart & Perkins, 2008).

Use Independent Assessment Items

If you are creating an assessment from scratch, you will want to ensure that quality, independent items are the foundation. *Independent* means that a student does not have to get one item right in order to get another item correct. For example, if an assessment first asks a student to graph the x and y intercept and then asks questions about the resulting graph, you will note complications because the student must first graph the x and y

intercept correctly, or the following responses will be incorrect. These kinds of items are known as *dependent*. The details of writing quality independent items are beyond the scope of this chapter, but they are very important. If necessary, review the literature on how to write solid constructed (short-answer, fill-in-the-blank, and essay) and selected-response (matching, multiple-choice, true/ false) items (Gareis & Grant, 2008). Often modifications can be made to existing assessment items with little time and expense, resulting in a fairer testing situation for students.

Setting Mastery and Cut Scores

Once you have connected items to varying proficiencies, consider how you can best score assessments. Start by asking, "Is it possible for me to create an assessment that everyone in my class could pass?" Then ask, "And is it possible for me to create an assessment that virtually no one could pass?" The answer to both questions is a resounding yes, because passing rates are dependent upon the difficulty of the assessment items. If the majority of items are at the advanced level of the PLD, the exam will likely be more difficult, and if the majority of items are at the beginning level of the PLD, the test will likely be easier. It is important to carefully consider item difficulty based upon the proficiency level descriptions. Certainly, the cut score for proficiency will be affected based upon the difficulty of the items. If there are more difficult items on the exam, the proficiency cut score will be lower than if there are many more beginning-level items. When an exam is too difficult, most students will not perform well. Some teachers will feel the need to lower their performance expectations and manipulate the grading scale to reflect the lower performance of the class results. Rather than use this compensating mentality, consider the difficulty of the items in the first place by comparing the assessment items to the PLD for that essential learning or standard. Adjusting the grading scale will not be necessary if items are created more accurately at the beginning of the process.

Once we understand that all tests are not created equally, trying to fit all types of assessment information (quizzes, tests, unit exams, semester tests) into one arbitrary grading scale seems absurd. Now we have the rationale for engaging further with evaluation and grading conversations and for figuring the cut scores for the varied proficiency levels. If a teacher administers a really difficult assessment and uses the same grading scale as for a much easier assessment, the teacher has skewed the evaluation results. Proficiency would not mean the same thing for the two assessments, especially if the teacher gives both assessments equal consideration in calculating grades (by the typical process of averaging scores).

Although there are numerous methods for figuring cut scores, one method applicable to classroom teachers is the modified Angoff method (Impara & Plake, 1998). This entails first creating PLDs as described earlier. Using an existing assessment, review each assessment item in comparison to the proficiency level description, and identify items accordingly. Determine if there are enough opportunities for *all* levels of proficiency to allow you to make a confident evaluation of actual performance. Three to five items or opportunities per level is a good rule of thumb for objective assessments. However, if the assessment has multiple-point items or writing samples, this number would not be necessary. You must always work to balance efficiency with effectiveness as you consider the type and number of assessment items. Work through the assessment item by item, determining what level of proficiency each item is and tallying the corresponding proficiency column (see table 5.1).

The modified Angoff method is appropriate for both objectively and subjectively scored assessments. *Objective assessments* have specific correct answers, as in multiple-choice, true/false, or matching tests. *Subjective assessments* require evaluating a project, a performance, an artwork, or a writing sample, meaning that there will be more variation in responses and more variability among assessors' evaluations. Teachers using the modified Angoff method must know both the assessment content and typical performance for students at that grade level. Teachers analyze each item on the assessment in relationship to student performance. The method is not sample group–size dependent; in other words, the size of the sample—small numbers of students or a large group of students—does not influence results. This is important because other methods for figuring cut scores often require a minimum of fifty students.

Steps in the Modified Angoff Method

Step 1

Look at the first assessment item. If you would expect the beginning students to answer item 1 correctly, put a "1" in this column. This denotes the item as a beginning level item. As you might guess, if beginning students would get this item correct, then barely progressing students would also get the assessment item correct, and so would the barely proficient and the barely advanced students. Place a "1" in both of these columns accordingly.

Table 5.1: Filling Out the Chart, Step 1

Assessment Item Number	Beginning	Barely Progressing	Barely Proficient	Barely Advanced
1.	1	1	1	1
2.				
3.				
4.				

Step 2

Review assessment item number 2. If a barely progressing student would miss this item, put a "0" in the blank. If a barely progressing student would miss the item, so would a beginning student. Then consider barely proficient students. If you would expect them to answer the item correctly, put a "1" in this column. Again, if barely proficient students would get the question correct, so would the barely advanced students. Place a "1" in this blank also (table 5.2).

Table 5.2: Filling Out the Chart, Step 2

Assessment Item Number	Beginning	Barely Progressing	Barely Proficient	Barely Advanced
1.	1	1	1	1
2.	0	0	1	1
3.				
4.				

Step 3

Review assessment item 3. If barely progressing students and barely proficient students would miss this item, put a "0" in both blanks, as well as for the beginning student. Then consider the barely advanced students. If you would expect them to answer the item correctly, put a "1" in this column (table 5.3).

Table 5.3: Filling Out the Chart, Step 3

Assessment Item Number	Beginning	Barely Progressing	Barely Proficient	Barely Advanced
1.	1	1	1	1
2.	0	0	1	1
3.	0	0	0	1
4.				

Step 4

Continue for all items. In reviewing assessment items, it would be possible to have a "0" in all columns, indicating that only students above a barely advanced level would get the item correct. This might also be the case if you find that the item is not well written and, therefore, no level of students would get this item correct. You will have to use empirical evidence (a sampling of students over time) to make this determination (table 5.4).

Table 5.4: Filling Out the Chart, Step 4

Assessment Item Number	Beginning	Barely Progressing	Barely Proficient	Barely Advanced
1.	1	1	1	1
2.	0	0	1	1
3.	0	0	0	1
4.	0	0	0	0

Step 5

Next, add up the number of points for each performance level, and record the sum at the bottom of each column. Then create a total possible point range for that column (the range should begin with the lowest possible number of correct items to score in that column and end with one less than the number of items correct in the next column [table 5.5]).

Table 5.5: Filling Out the Chart, Step 5

Assessment Item Number	Beginning	Barely Progressing	Barely Proficient	Barely Advanced
1.	1	1	1	1
2.	0	0	1	1
3.	0	0	0	1
4.	0	0	0	0
5.	0	1	1	1
6.	0	0	1	1
7.	0	0	1	1
8.	0	0	0	1
9.	1	1	1	1
10.	0	0	0	1
Item/Point Totals	0–2	3–5	6–8	9–10

Table 5.5 shows your cut scores and your mastery ranges. For example, 3 is the cut score where the progressing level begins, 6 is the cut score for proficient, and 9 for advanced. The range for each proficiency level is what's called the *mastery level* or *mastery range* (Angoff, 1971). The mastery range on table 5.5 is 3–5 for progressing, 6–8 for proficient, and 9–10 for advanced. Some assessment items may be worth multiple points. For questions worth multiple points, divide the points among levels, allocating the number of points that a student barely at that level would be likely to get correct (Nebraska Department of Education, 2007). On a 4-point item, for example, if a student gets 1 point out of four, the student would be at the beginning level; 2 or 3 points might put the student at the progressing level, and all 4 points would put the student at proficiency. The mastery range denotes the continuum of proficiency within each PLD category. So according to table 5.5, a student can be considered proficient who earns 6 points or gets six assessment items correct, and also with up to 8. Once a student gets 9 or more points or assessment items correct, he or she is now in the advanced mastery range.

Determining Grades

The process of creating proficiency level descriptions and using them to determine grades helps us initiate stimulating and coherent professional conversations about how students obtain competency. As colleagues, we must discuss and agree upon the critical skill sets within our particular content areas. As we create PLDs for those skill sets, our conversations with colleagues, students, and parents begin to sound different. We start to wonder first what *proficient* means for each exam or skill set, and then what grade, mark, or score that level of proficiency should receive. This is an entirely different conversation than making grading tasks fit into the varied grading scales used across North America. Discussions with students and parents can then focus more on the degree of learning the student has achieved and the challenges that remain ahead and less on the percentage or letter grade received. Students and parents become clearer about the knowledge and skills needed to obtain the varied levels of proficiency and consequently can make informed adjustments without "guessing" what the teacher expects.

The Challenge of Changing Our Practice

There seems to be little argument among college professors or in the workforce as to the skill sets most important for students, which include critical thinking, analytical reasoning, and problem solving (Wagner, 2008; Partnership for 21st Century Learning, 2003). However, there are many complex perspectives on how we should score student work and report such information. As Thomas Guskey noted back in 1996, "Grading practices are not the result of careful thought or sound evidence; rather, they are used because teachers experienced these practices as students and, having little training or experience with other options, continue their use" (p. 16). Ken O'Connor (2002) challenges us to consider grading practices that are accurate, consistent, meaningful, and supportive of learning.

As we further our conversations about consistency and coherence in grading practices, we must continue with in-depth reading and researching of this topic, and we must engage all levels, preschool through higher education, in such thinking, discussing, and learning. Many states are embarking upon preschool through undergraduate or graduate school conversations about competency expectations. It would be beneficial to extend these discussions to evaluation as well. Teacher leaders are our best allies for instigating the conversations and facilitating the development of valid and reliable assessment and evaluation systems. We must get beyond grade point average (GPA) and class rank (a normed indicator completely dependent upon the abilities of the students within a graduating class and all of the variations in our current GPAs) and work toward using more portfolios of actual performance samples and other indicators of knowledge and abilities.

In furthering this imperative work of improving grading practices, an understanding of change will serve us well. Michael Fullan, an international authority on education reform, illuminated the unknown possibilities of change when he stated:

> Change is a double-edged sword. The change process occurs at an inconsistent pace and raises the level of anxiety in everyone impacted by the change. Yet when things are unsettled, it is a prime opportunity to move forward and create breakthroughs not possible in stagnant societies. (2001, p. 1)

When embarking on the creation and implementation of a new grading system for your school or teacher team, it is important to be sensitive to the different degrees of readiness among team members. Teachers' current grading practices will determine how and when to introduce the different steps along a continuum of improvement (see fig. 5.3). Some small changes can probably be made right away in single classrooms. More dramatic changes require teachers to engage in more systemic conversations and probably will entail developing new policies and procedures for consistent implementation across a team, school, or district.

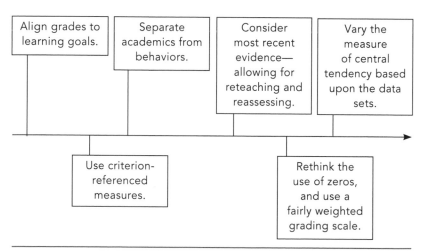

Figure 5.3: A continuum of changing assessment and grading practices (adapted from O'Connor, 2002).

On the beginning side of implementation, teachers might align their grading with standards and learning goals, using criterion-referenced targets in order to ensure the possibility for all students to be successful. As staff assessment literacy deepens, teacher leaders can encourage colleagues to separate student behaviors and work habits from academic grades (Marzano, 2000; O'Connor, 2002). Allow time for colleagues to work through these phases and gain confidence before expecting all of the grading practices to change. As staff philosophies begin to evolve toward more student-centered and standards-based grading practices, ease colleagues further along the continuum of changing practices. You might, for example, discuss the rationale for considering the most recent evidence and changing grades as students demonstrate increased learning—what O'Connor (2002) calls "grading in pencil."

Rethink Zeros

Maintaining the momentum of the change implementation, examine the unfairness and poor practice of giving zeros—of assuming that students know nothing because their assignments are overdue or missing. This is not to say that such lack of student responsibility should be encouraged; it certainly should not be. However, we must separate student work habits from their academic achievement. Guskey and Bailey (2001) argue that giving zeros is one of the most controversial and unfair practices in which we engage. A zero is six times more powerful than any other grade (assuming a typical ten-point grade band in which 90–100 = A) when averaging. A zero is worth sixty "negative" points (it is earned for anything from 0–60 points), while an A is only worth ten "positive" points (it is earned only for 90–100 points). As many students already know, they cannot make up such a discrepancy within a quarter, trimester, or even a semester; a single zero has a traumatic effect on a grade calculated using averaging. If the median is used as the measure of central tendency, however, zeros are not so impactful, as the median calculation excludes outlier scores.

It has almost become amusing to hear some of us complain about low levels of student motivation, and yet many of us continue to engage in such unfair and harmful evaluation practices. There are at least three measures of central tendency appropriate for mathematically calculating scores for students. Most state mathematics standards for fifth grade, for example, address mean, median, and mode, yet many of us rely solely on the average (the mean) for calculating a grade, mark, or grade-point average (Gravetter & Wallnau, 2004).

Select an Appropriate Measure of Central Tendency

Most teachers rely on using a measure of central tendency for figuring grades. Deciding which measure of central tendency to use should be completely dependent upon the data set of student scores. For example, if the data set contains *outliers*—extreme scores compared to the rest of the data set—the median or mode is the better measure to use, as it discounts the outliers. This is certainly another great topic for conversation. Ask colleagues to consider when to use the various measures of central tendency (mean, median, and mode) and why they might choose to do so; their answers will highlight our over-reliance on the mean and our use of manipulative practices (such as dropping the highest and lowest scores) to make using the mean more palatable. Why not use the median as the more appropriate measure when outliers exist? Table 5.6 shows three identical data sets for a student's work over a grading term, each set scored with a different measure of central tendency. Notice that on most grading scales, the student's possible grade would range from a C (for the mean) to an A (the mode).

Table 5.6: Variations in Grade Calculation by Measure of Central Tendency

Mean: 78.57	Median: 90	Mode: 100
100	100	100
100	100	100
100	100	100
90	90	90
80	80	80
80	80	80
0	0	0

The most important thing to keep in mind is that evaluation is the judgment made about student performance after accounting for a body of evidence. Some students take more time to become proficient. Therefore, is it okay for students to retake exams and receive the later grade (rather than an average of their first and later grades)? If we are more concerned about student learning than about teacher content coverage, the answer should be yes, and calculating a measure of central tendency will not be necessary. Often teachers are apprehensive about what many assessment gurus call the *residual retention* of tested items from a previous assessment. That is, they worry that students who retake the same exam might remember the questions even if they have not truly acquired new learning. Although this can be a concern for reading passages, it is rarely as much of an issue as one might think. In fact, with all of the item banks available to us, why not create a different form of the assessment with new items? That way, students have multiple opportunities to demonstrate proficiency, yet the test items vary from the original assessment. Many teachers also require students to provide evidence of learning before they are given an additional testing opportunity. This motivates students to achieve a deeper understanding of the content.

Where Do I Start?

As educators, we must continue to challenge ourselves as the lifelong learners we profess to be. Therefore, as we learn new information and read the research on student achievement and motivation, we are obligated to make important improvements to our practice. As the old riddle goes, "How do you eat an elephant? One bite at a time." Taking any step toward coherence and consistency in the development and refinement of our assessment and grading practices is admirable.

Begin with your own classroom, and take small steps to improve. Malcolm Gladwell (2000, p. 142) notes, "Poor practice can be reversed and tipped by the tinkering with the smallest of details of the immediate environment." Consider the grading improvement continuum, find a place you feel comfortable starting to revise your practice, and then do it. As you conduct your own action research within your classroom, students will undoubtedly note a new, refreshing perspective. You might also start by reviewing a few of your frequently used assessments. Do you have PLDs that clearly articulate your expectations? Have you reviewed your assessment items or performance opportunities to ensure chances for students at varying levels of proficiency to clearly and fairly demonstrate their abilities? These are but a few places to begin these profound changes.

Next, share your commitment. As Gladwell points out, "Epidemics tip because of the extraordinary efforts of a few select carriers" (2000, p. 22). Work with others at your grade level or in your content area. Build critical mass. Be one of the select few. As Gandhi said, "Be the change you wish to see in the world."

References and Resources

Ainsworth, L. (2003). *Power standards: Identifying the standards that matter most.* Englewood, CO: Advanced Learning.

American Educational Research Association (AERA), American Psychological Association (APA), National Council on Measurement in Education (NCME) Joint Committee. (1999). *Standards for educational and psychological testing.* Washington, DC: American Educational Research Association.

Angoff, W. H. (1971). Scales, norms and equivalent scores. In R. L. Thorndike (Ed.), *Educational Measurement* (2nd ed., pp. 508–600). Washington, DC: American Council on Education.

Berk, R. A. (1986). A consumer's guide to setting performance standards on criterion-referenced tests. *Review of Educational Research, 56*(1), 137–172.

Berk, R. A. (1995). Something old, something new, something borrowed, a lot to do! *Applied Measurement in Education, 8*(1), 99–109.

Berk, R. A. (1996). Standard setting: The next generation (Where few psychometricians have gone before!). *Applied Measurement in Education, 9*(3), 215–235.

Bloom, B. S., & Krathwohl, D. R. (1956). *Taxonomy of educational objectives: The classification of educational goals, by a committee of college and university examiners. Handbook 1: Cognitive domain.* New York: Longmans.

Boss, T. (2005). *An educator's perception of STARS from selected Nebraska assessment coordinators.* Unpublished doctoral dissertation, University of Nebraska-Lincoln. Accessed at http://digitalcommons.unl.edu/dissertations/AAI3194108/ on December 27, 2008.

Brennan, R. L., & Lockwood, R. E. (1980). A comparison of the Nedelsky and Angoff cutting score procedures using generalizability theory. *Applied Psychological Measurement, 4*(2), 219–240.

Buckendahl, C. W., Impara, J. C., & Plake, B. S. (2002, Winter). District accountability without a state assessment: A proposed model. *Educational Measurement, 21*(4), 6–16.

Colorado Department of Education. (2008). *Standards and assessments.* Accessed at www.cde.state.co.us/cdeassess/documents/csap/csap_plds.html on September 24, 2008.

Endorf, D. P. (2005). *An educator's perception of STARS from selected Nebraska teachers.* Unpublished doctoral dissertation, University of Nebraska-Lincoln. Accessed at http://digitalcommons.unl.edu/dissertations/AAI3201765/ on December 27, 2008.

Fullan, M. (2001). *Leading in a culture of change.* San Francisco: Jossey-Bass.

Gareis, C., & Grant, L. (2008). *Teacher-made assessments: How to connect curriculum, instruction, and learning.* Larchmont, NY: Eye on Education.

Gladwell, M. (2000). *The tipping point: How little things can make a big difference.* Boston: Little, Brown and Company.

Gravetter, F., & Wallnau, L. (2004). *Statistics for the behavioral sciences* (6th ed.). Belmont, CA: Wadsworth/Thompson Learning.

Guskey, T. R. (1994). Making the grade: What benefits students? *Educational Leadership, 52*(2), 14–20.

Guskey, T. R. (Ed.). (1996). *Communicating student learning: 1996 yearbook of the Association for Supervision and Curriculum Development.* Alexandria, VA: Association for Supervision and Curriculum Development.

Guskey, T. & Bailey, J. (Eds.). (2001). *Developing grading and reporting systems for student learning.* Thousand Oaks, CA: Corwin.

Heflebower, T. (2005). *An educator's perception of STARS from selected Nebraska education service unit staff developers.* Unpublished doctoral dissertation, University of Nebraska-Lincoln. Accessed at http://digitalcommons.unl.edu/dissertations/AAI3194116/ on December 27, 2008.

Impara, J. C., & Plake, B. S. (1997). Standard setting: An alternative approach. *Journal of Educational Measurement, 34*(4), 353–366.

Impara, J. C., & Plake, B. S. (1998). Teachers' ability to estimate item difficulty: A test of the assumptions in the Angoff standard setting method. *Journal of Educational Measurement, 35*(1), 69–81.

Marzano, R. (2000). *Transforming classroom grading.* Alexandria, VA: Association for Supervision and Curriculum Development.

Marzano, R., & Kendall, J. (2007). *The new taxonomy of educational objectives.* Thousand Oaks, CA: Corwin.

Nebraska Department of Education. (2007). *Guidelines and requirements for documenting assessment quality for STARS.* Accessed at www.nde.state.ne.us/assessment/STARSSummary.html on October 28, 2008.

O'Connor, K. (2002). *How to grade for learning: Linking grades to standards* (2nd ed.). Thousand Oaks, CA: Corwin.

Partnership for 21st Century Learning. (2003, June). *Learning for the 21st century: A report and MILE guide for 21st century skills.* Accessed at www.21stcenturyskills.org/images/stories/otherdocs/P21_Report.pdf on October 28, 2008.

Plake, B. S., Impara, J. C., & Irwin, P. M. (2000). Consistency of Angoff–based predictions of item performance: Evidence of technical quality of results from the Angoff standard setting method. *Journal of Educational Measurement, 37*(4), 347–355.

Reid, J. (1991). Training judges to generate standard-setting data. *Educational Measurement: Issues & Practice, 10*(2), 11–14.

Ritchhart, R., & Perkins, D. (2008). Making thinking visible. *Educational Leadership, 65*(5), 57–61.

Stiggins, R. J., Arter, J., Chappuis, J., & Chappuis, S. (2006). *Classroom assessment for student learning: Doing it right—Using it well.* Portland, OR: Educational Testing Service.

Wagner, A. (2008). *Global achievement gap.* New York: Basic Books.

Warrick, P. (2005). *An educator's perception of STARS from selected Nebraska principals.* Unpublished doctoral dissertation, University of Nebraska-Lincoln. Accessed at http://digitalcommons.unl.edu/dissertations/AAI3194129/ on December 27, 2008.

ADAM YOUNG

Adam Young is the principal of White Pine High School (WPHS) in Ely, Nevada. Named Administrator of the Year by the Nevada Association of School Boards, Adam enjoys working for his alma mater, leading both students and teachers toward high levels of learning. In the years since Adam has served as principal, WPHS students and staff have achieved numerous honors. The school has earned either High Achieving or Exemplary status from the Nevada Department of Education since 2003. In 2006 and 2008, WPHS was recognized as a Nevada Model School. Additionally, Adam and the WPHS team were recognized by the International Center for Leadership in Education for creating a National Model School in 2007.

SIX

Using Common Assessments in Uncommon Courses

Adam Young

A great deal of research has been done in recent years on the topic of assessment. One theme specifically has earned significant time in the spotlight: formative assessment. *Formative assessment* was defined by Paul Black and Dylan Wiliam (1998) as "all those activities undertaken by teachers and/or by students which provide information to be used as feedback to modify the teaching and learning activities in which they engage" (pp. 7–8). Black and Wiliam found that formative assessment impacts students' performance more than anything else. Robert Marzano calls formative assessment "one of the most powerful weapons in a teacher's arsenal" (2006, p. 2). Rick Stiggins observes, "Assessment *for* learning [that is, formative assessment] rivals one-on-one tutoring in its effectiveness" (Stiggins, Arter, Chappuis, & Chappuis, 2004, p. 27). Clearly, formative assessment is a powerful instrument to help students learn at higher levels.

The impact of formative assessments can be even greater, however, when they are developed and administered commonly (Schmoker, 2004). *Common formative assessments* require teachers to agree upon what they will teach, what they will assess, and how and when they will administer assessments. Common formative assessments demand discussion about the best ways to help students learn the agreed-upon outcomes. They require consensus regarding the best way for students to demonstrate their learning. Stiggins states that teachers "benefit from the union of their wisdom about how to help students continue to grow as learners" (2005, p. 82). Mike Schmoker concludes that "common, teacher-made, formative assessments . . . inform productive adjustments to instruction but also ensure consistently delivered, viable curriculum as they allow teams to see, on a frequent basis, that their efforts are paying off" (2006, p. 123). Robert Marzano (2006) quantifies these efforts in statistical terms, noting that common formative assessments can achieve a reliability coefficient of .82 (matching that of some state tests), thereby helping ensure consistency among teachers in assessment practices. Finally, Larry Ainsworth and Donald Viegut (2006) assert that developing and scoring these student assessments is one of the most powerful forms of professional development available to teachers.

Clearly, the practice of administering common formative assessments to students helps improve their learning as well as the learning of their teachers. Doug Reeves goes so far as to say that they are "essential for all schools" (2006, p. ix). But what happens when schools and teams are too small to adopt this practice? What happens when there are only two or three English teachers in a building, and they all teach different courses? What about fine arts teachers in larger schools? Usually there are only a few, and the content they teach is different. What about career and technical education (CTE) teachers in large and small schools who encounter similar hurdles in teaching different content?

In discussion with other professionals, I often hear they are frustrated that they don't seem to be able to make the practice work because of barriers like small school size; their teachers perceive common formative assessments as either not relevant to them or as too difficult to integrate effectively. However, a careful review of the research noted in the last few paragraphs reveals that while common formative assessments are perhaps most easily accomplished in courses of identical content, there is no evidence stating that they are not *also* a valid and truly effective way for teachers of uncommon courses to improve student learning. In fact, none of the researchers cited earlier limits the use of common formative assessments to courses of identical content. If using formative assessments has been described as producing gains "amongst the largest ever reported for educational intervention" (Black & Wiliam, 1998, p. 61), and common assessments are a must for all schools (Reeves, 2006), why can't students in all courses experience these gains, even though their teacher may be the only choir, government, world history, algebra 2, or auto technology teacher on staff?

This chapter will outline a common assessment process that teachers of uncommon courses in any setting can use to collaboratively focus on student learning. In addition to outlining the process, the chapter will provide an in-depth case study of a small rural high school as an example of how the strategies work in the lives of practitioners. While the case study comes from one particular school, the steps can be adapted to fit any circumstance.

The Process

Step 1: Form Teams

First, teachers form teams, even if they do not teach identical courses, based on what they *do* have in common. This can look very different depending on the situation. For example, in a small elementary school, teachers might form a K–5 vertical team. In larger middle and high schools, teachers might form a fine arts team consisting of choir, band, drama, and orchestra teachers. A CTE team could consist of construction, auto technology, welding, agriculture, business, and family and consumer sciences teachers. In smaller middle and high schools, teachers might form interdisciplinary teams or like-content teams. For example, the English team might consist of the ninth-grade English, tenth-grade English, American literature, and British literature teachers, even if there is only one of each. Similarly, the science team might consist of four teachers: biology, chemistry and physics, health occupations, and environmental science.

Step 2: Identify Common Denominators

Teams must then begin the challenge of determining what their common denominators are. Not surprisingly, common formative assessments must assess something that is common. Therefore, teachers must begin the dialogue of determining what their commonalities are. Agreeing upon content as the common denominator is difficult since the team members' subjects are diverse. Therefore, teachers must agree upon common skills they expect their students to achieve. An English team might agree upon common skills and mastery levels for reading, writing, and language usage. A social studies team might define common skills essential to their discipline—skills such as asking questions to seek out pertinent information, determining cause-and-effect relationships, and distinguishing fact from opinion. A science team might agree upon skills such as interpreting data from charts and graphs, making inferences, hypothesizing, or scientific inquiry. An interdisciplinary team might agree upon the skills of knowing how to learn or how to take effective notes. Of course, the knowledge and skills unique to a particular course or academic discipline must continue to be assessed in individual classes; the common assessments allow teachers to reinforce only those knowledge and skills that are common.

Identifying common denominators is crucial to moving forward. This best occurs when team members first clarify in writing the content-specific outcomes for their courses. Once this is done, team members can consult with one another to find common goals. If teachers are teamed according to like-content areas, finding common ground will not be as challenging. These teams can refer to standards published by their content organizations such as the National Council of Teachers of Mathematics. Frequently, teachers in this process find themselves looking to school improvement goals to find common ground. Most schools have these goals—for example, raising students' performance on language arts tests. This is a reasonable common denominator that an English team can adopt. Similarly, most schools have goals that deal with helping students become better thinkers and users of information. This is a logical goal for social studies and science teams to adopt. Many middle schools have global goals that include helping students internalize learning. This can be a common denominator for teachers in any content area.

A bit more creativity might be required for teams with members from different content areas, such as CTE and music. However, it is important to remember that many students are motivated to attend school because of their love for programs like these. This gives teachers on CTE and music teams great power to influence their students not only in learning content, but in becoming lifelong learners. These team members must understand that their role is just as crucial as that of core-subject teachers. A music team might choose goals related to reflecting on performance. A CTE team might decide that the skills of reading for information, describing step-by-step processes, and communicating effectively are essential regardless of the specific course.

Step 3: Select Most Important Outcomes

Reeves (2002) contends that it is better to assess a small number of essential skills of exceeding importance than to assess many skills. Similarly, administering common assessments in uncommon courses works best by choosing one or two most important common outcomes and measuring students' progress over time based on these outcomes. Therefore, once team members have agreed on what they have in common, the next step is to choose the most important common outcomes and consent to base the common assessments on those outcomes. Typically, outcomes chosen for the common assessments link to other school improvement initiatives. For example, if literacy is a schoolwide goal, teams (regardless of their content) can develop common outcomes based on literacy and use them as the focus for common assessment. Such outcomes might sound like the following: "Students will write to persuade an audience" or "Students will read informational text and summarize key points."

Step 4: Select a Method of Assessment

Next, team members must select a method of assessment that will best measure the selected skill. This can pose a slight problem if team members are locked into traditional multiple-choice pencil-and-paper tests. In *Classroom Assessment* for *Student Learning* (2004), Rick Stiggins, Judith Arter, Jan Chappuis, and Steve Chappuis describe the importance of matching the assessment method with the target to be assessed; best practice for measuring students' mastery of skills and outcomes as described in Steps 2 and 3 is *not* using selected response or multiple choice. This dilemma provides yet more opportunity for building shared knowledge among team members. A collective study of research on assessment can help team members determine what type of assessment best measures their desired outcomes. This process of developing and scoring student assessments is an extremely meaningful and powerful method of professional development, as noted by Schmoker (2004), Stiggins (2005), and Ainsworth (2007). This type of professional development is sustained and embedded by a continuous process of study and application.

To begin this process, teachers might look at effective assessment methods using Stiggins' work. They would find that measuring skills usually requires some type of performance assessment. While measuring progress toward a schoolwide literacy goal such as "Students will read informational text and summarize key points" could be accomplished through multiple-choice testing, actually requiring the students to do the summarizing would be a better assessment match. Therefore, a more open-ended assessment would be needed. Similarly, measuring progress toward a schoolwide literacy goal of "Students will write to persuade an audience" would be almost impossible to accomplish through a multiple-choice test. Students would need to create a sample of persuasive writing in order for their skill to be truly assessed.

Step 5: Develop a Rubric

Once the team has agreed on a method of assessing the skill, members must develop a rubric that clarifies targets and performance levels and communicates them to students. The rubric must contain a section for content (which is different depending on the class) and for the skill being measured. Many powerful discussions among teachers result when they consider the criteria by which they judge student work. This is true when course content is identical, but it is also true when teachers of diverse courses have agreed-upon common skills their students need to learn:

> When teachers work together to establish criteria for judging their students' work, set standards, and make group decisions, the collaboration has many spin-offs. . . . They tend to enhance one another's understanding of instruction and curriculum, develop agreement about the nature and quality of the instruments and approaches for assessing their students' work, challenge and question their own expectations for students, and develop more confidence in their decisions and in their accountability to the outside community. (Earl & LeMahieu, 1997, p. 166)

Deep, rich dialogue and a better understanding of the skills students are expected to master result when teams engage in these conversations.

Step 6: Develop Anchors

Once this learning among team members takes place, teachers are ready to develop *anchors*—examples and nonexamples—to use in the learning process with students. The anchors should be developed based on the type of assessment chosen, as discussed in Step 4. These anchors might be extended written-response samples, videos, demonstrations, or performance-based models. The key is that anchors model what is expected of students and are linked to the rubric developed in Step 5. These anchors can be used to teach students not only content, but the agreed-upon common skill as well. Their development leads to discussions within the team about the best way to help students reach mastery.

Step 7: Teach the Assessment Format

The next step is to teach students the format of the common assessment, keeping in mind that the content will be different among the various courses. The goal in this system of common assessments is to help students achieve mastery of the common skill. In a CTE team, the common assessment might be designed to help students refine their ability to describe a step-by-step process. Therefore, each common assessment requires them to do this. It follows that if team members want students to make progress in this skill, then they will share the rubric and anchors with students frequently. Students need to know that they are being assessed both on their content knowledge (whether auto technology, health occupations, business and marketing, or family and consumer sciences) and on the skill of giving step-by-step directions. They should see and practice with the anchors *before* the common assessment is given. As the semester progresses and teachers administer further common assessments, students should again review the anchors.

Step 8: Administer and Score the Assessment

After students have been exposed to the anchors, team members should administer the first common assessment. They should communicate to students that the assessment is to help team members measure students' skill levels and also to inform team members of their success in teaching the skill. Team members then gather the responses and meet together to score the assessments, using the rubric created in Step 5. This helps promote consistency in grading. Scores are organized and reported based on each student's performance on each area of the rubric. Averages may also be reported, but the focus must be on analyzing how many students met each of the criteria addressed on the rubric.

Step 9: Use the Results to Adjust Instruction

Each of the preceding steps is essential to the process—but none is more important than Step 9. The strategies discussed in this chapter are not the end but the means to the end. In other words, going through this process just for the sake of giving common assessments has little value. The true value lies in what happens after the common assessments are given. What do teachers do with results? What adjustments do they make in the classroom? How is the learning of students affected?

First, teachers must determine what the results mean. Usually there are trends that indicate a class's areas of strength and weakness. Teachers must organize the data in a way that allows them to see these trends. Teachers learn indirectly about their performance; they also learn how they compare with their colleagues. Most important, however, is that they learn where exactly their students fall. This leads to structured and organized discussions about adjustments in the classroom. Teachers might begin this discussion by having a colleague model a mini-lesson. The team could also collectively research proven methods of teaching the agreed-upon skill. Peer observations might follow, in which teachers take turns observing and supporting one another while implementing instructional changes in the classroom. The result is that on the next common assessment, student learning is affected in a positive way. Then the crucial process of Step 9 begins again.

Common formative assessments are an excellent way to focus the work of collaborative teams. Richard DuFour, Rebecca DuFour, and Robert Eaker (2008) state:

> When schools ensure every teacher has been engaged in a process to clarify what students are to learn and how their learning will be assessed, they promote the clarity essential to effective teaching. When teachers have access to each other's ideas, methods, and materials, they can expand their repertoire of skills. (p. 215)

They also contend that team members who engage in the strategies described in this chapter develop their own "assessment literacy" (p. 215). This process of building the capacity of teachers by using common formative assessments is too important and effective to limit to only teams who teach identical courses or content. A strategy that influences student learning positively more than nearly any other practice (Black & Wiliam, 1998) is worthy of the time and energy of all teachers, regardless of their content area and the size of the school in which they teach.

Case Study

The social studies team at White Pine High School consists of four members—a government teacher (who also teaches French), a U.S. history teacher (who also teaches world history and health), a world history teacher (who also teaches U.S. history and German), and a special education teacher whose background is in social studies. These teachers organized themselves as a like-content team after studying the research on professional learning communities; several members of the team researched the impact of common formative assessments on student learning and decided to build their collective and individual assessment capacity.

The school had only 420 students, and so the teachers knew that their challenge would be adapting, while simultaneously implementing with fidelity, the common-assessment approach.

Because their courses were diverse, the team decided to articulate a common set of essential outcomes. The school schedule for students extended the school day four days per week and banked the time. On Wednesdays, students left early, which allowed teachers and the social studies team time within the contract day to do the work. Over a period of several months, the team developed a list of skill- and thinking-based essential outcomes, including the following:

- Students will distinguish fact from opinion.

- Students will synthesize information.

- Students will demonstrate effective note-taking skills.

- Students will make and defend an argument.

- Students will take information from the past and relate it to today.

Members of the team agreed that these outcomes would be areas of common focus in addition to individual course content. They listed these outcomes on their course syllabi and made posters with graphic representations for their classrooms. They agreed to model each of the skills in their classrooms whenever possible and to point out to students when the skills were being used.

Next, the social studies team began discussions about which of the common outcomes were most important and should be the focus of their common assessments. After a series of team meetings in which team members built shared knowledge and gained better understanding of the common outcomes, they selected the goal of synthesizing information. They chose this outcome as the most important through discussions of the vast amount of material sometimes covered in courses. Team members felt that if they could help their students master the skill of synthesizing information, then the systems thinking needed to excel in social studies would follow. Moreover, one of the school improvement goals was to develop students' thinking and reasoning skills.

Since their state did not use a social studies exit exam to directly monitor their efforts, the team members decided that they could best contribute to schoolwide efforts by helping students learn to synthesize information. They brought in articles and research about synthesizing to deepen their understanding of the skill. Eventually, they more clearly defined this goal in student-friendly language as "being able to identify and give the significance of related events, people, or concepts, and then being able to explain how the events, people, or concepts fit together."

The team members researched the best way for students to demonstrate the skill of synthesis. They believed in the theory of "learning by doing." In other words, they thought they would learn more through trial and error than through trying to perfect the assessment process before beginning. Therefore, they began by developing and administering a multiple-choice test. They learned after one attempt that this format would not allow students to think at the deep level they desired. Next, the team members tried an essay format. After one attempt with this format, they learned that it was probably a little too unstructured and students needed some more clearly defined guidelines. Finally, the teachers agreed on a modified extended written-response format. They decided to invent their own extended-response item that measured exactly what they wanted their students to do and called this assessment the Triad Response. Using the essential outcome just noted, team members collaboratively agreed upon several keys that would help students demonstrate their understanding of the outcome. In world history, the team decided upon several sets of three related terms. In U.S. history and government, the team did the same thing. After agreeing upon the terms to use in each course, team members presented the appropriate sets to the students in their respective courses. They asked students to write one paragraph about each term, identifying it and explaining its significance, for a total of three paragraphs. In a fourth and final paragraph, students had to explain how all three of the terms were related and their collective impact (see table 6.1).

Table 6.1: Two Sets of Triad Response Terms for a Social Studies Common Assessment

Government	U.S. History	World History
Supreme Court	Abraham Lincoln	Republic
John Marshall	Slavery	Rome
Judicial review	Emancipation Proclamation	United States
Checks and balances	George W. Bush	Scientific Revolution
Federalism	Iraq	Enlightenment
Constitution	Oil	Sir Isaac Newton

The team members developed four common assessments in the same format that they would give throughout the semester. While the content was different among classes, the essential skill being measured—synthesis—stayed the same. This approach allowed team members to focus on a common denominator and assess it over time.

Team members shared with one another research on formative assessment from Stiggins and Marzano. They learned that formative assessment exists so that both students and teachers can improve. They learned through this research that in order to effectively focus students' efforts on the right things, those right things must be defined. Therefore, they met together over a series of weeks and developed a rubric that laid out the criteria they would use to judge their students' work. The rubric included sections for content, synthesizing, transitioning between terms, and grammar and usage. They agreed that the score 4 would represent *mastery*, 3 would represent *proficiency*, 2 would represent *not yet*, and 1 would represent *emerging*. They then wrote anchor papers that exemplified each performance level. This deepened team members' understanding of the rubric's criteria.

Next, social studies team members integrated the anchor papers and rubrics into their content teaching. It is important to note that they did not take time away from their content as they taught students the criteria; instead, they used the content of their courses to teach students the skill of synthesizing. They gave students opportunities to practice and receive peer and teacher feedback using the criteria. Team members referred to the anchor papers regularly as students practiced the common skill through course content. Before they ever gave the first common assessment, team members talked with their students about the importance of the skill and how their sustained efforts through the semester would help them better understand the skill and work toward mastery.

Finally, team members gave the first common assessment. They felt strongly that using the common formative assessment approach had already improved their classroom focus on students' skill in synthesizing. However, they also learned that using the Triad Response had an unexpected benefit: their units were more focused on systems thinking than on details. Additionally, their units were driven with the end in mind—the end being that students would have both the content knowledge and skill level required to successfully complete a Triad Response. Even so, the team knew that formative assessments, even if they occur at the end of a unit, are designed for students to receive feedback. Therefore, they committed to giving students the opportunity to improve upon their work, regardless of the grade assigned to the initial response.

Team members collected the common assessments and scored them together during team time. Since all were social studies teachers, they shared the papers; each team member scored each paper, even though they did not all teach the same courses. Scoring the papers was a time-consuming task at first. Despite their previous discussions about the rubric and anchor papers, team members learned that they were not all scoring similarly. This led to short discussions as team members explained their rationales. With time, the scores became more consistent.

The reporting process focused teachers' attention on each student's progress and on helping all students learn, as opposed to being satisfied with students' average performance. Each teacher kept a record sheet—a final report—for his or her students. Table 6.2 (page 150) depicts student performance on each criterion. It also reports the students' aggregate score, which the team defined as "the score most frequently earned"—that is, the mode (rather than the average). The team was attempting to move away from averages as a scoring method. The aggregate score was less important than the individual skills measured.

While teachers were not required to share their results in this format with each other, they ended up doing so anyway. They learned that one teacher's students consistently outscored the rest. This teacher had the opportunity to share her expertise with her colleagues about how she helped her students understand the skill. She modeled a mini lesson for her team members and provided them with the materials to teach the skill as they prepared for the next common assessment.

Team members were not overly concerned about students' immediate proficiency; rather, they established their goal as students' gaining proficiency on the agreed-upon skills by the end of the semester.

Several weeks later, team members administered their second common assessment (again, using different content-related terms, but assessing the same skill). Each teacher noticed improvements in his or her students' responses. However, because the team members were focused on helping each student achieve his or her potential, they still analyzed the responses in the same way. They noticed that the content scores across the board were better, but the synthesis scores remained flat. Team members again sought out best practices in teaching the skill. They learned that organizing the information graphically and giving students a chance to talk through the synthesis stage with partners helped.

Table 6.2: Final Report: Student Scores From Teacher 1

	Content	Synthesis	Transitions	Grammar and Usage	TOTAL
Student 1	3	3	2	3	3
Student 2	4	4	4	3	4
Student 3	2	3	2	2	2
Student 4	4	2	2	2	2
Student 5	3	2	3	3	3
Student 6	2	2	2	2	2
TOTAL	Four students met the proficiency score of 3 or better.	Three students met the proficiency score of 3 or better.	Two students met the proficiency score of 3 or better.	Three students met the proficiency score of 3 or better.	Three students met the proficiency score of 3 or better.
SUMMARY	Thirty-three percent of students met the standard. Thirty-three percent of students exceeded the standard.	Thirty-three percent of students met the standard. Seventeen percent of students exceeded the standard.	Seventeen percent of students met the standard. Seventeen percent of students exceeded the standard.	Fifty percent of students met the standard. Zero percent of students exceeded the standard.	Thirty-three percent of students met the standard. Seventeen percent of students exceeded the standard.

They agreed to incorporate these two strategies regularly before the next common assessment. After planning mini-lessons around these two strategies, team members agreed to visit each other's classrooms to observe these strategies being used. They understood that using these strategies had to be purposeful rather than random and wanted to give and receive feedback about the best ways to use the strategies.

The team members administered the next common assessment with new terms three weeks later. Upon analyzing the data, they learned that 88 percent of their students had achieved proficiency or better as defined by their rubric. This meant that students had not only learned the content, but had greatly improved in their skill of synthesizing information—the outcome the social studies team had identified as most important.

At the end of the semester, team members administered the last common assessment. They had used each of the previous common assessments formatively to help themselves and their students understand where improvement was necessary. Team members asked their students to set goals in each criterion identified on the rubric. By this time, students were very familiar with how their work would be judged. Moreover, team members had spent time outside of class working with the 12 percent of students who had not yet reached proficiency using still more strategies identified during collective inquiry. These students knew that because the goal was to achieve proficiency at some point during the semester, but not necessarily at the same time everyone else did, their previous attempts would not be held against them—those were learning experiences. They were very motivated to reach their goal, as were the other students, many of whom were striving toward mastery.

The assessment was administered and results reported. Of all the students assessed, 96 percent met the standard (scoring 3 or better), and 55 percent exceeded the standard (scoring 4).

Through this process, all begun by the practice of administering common formative assessments, the team members engaged in relevant job-embedded professional development by studying curriculum to determine common essential skills, researching assessment, writing their own assessments, and planning, carrying out, and observing effective instructional strategies.

Summary

This chapter began by noting that research on common formative assessments does not limit the practice to courses of identical content. While it is certainly easier to craft common assessments when content is identical, it is worth the extra thought and effort to adapt the practice to courses of dissimilar content as well. The steps and the case study are offered as examples of how schools seeking the benefits associated with common assessments can adapt the practice and make it work. The learning experienced by teachers is not easily quantified but includes increased efficacy in matters of curriculum, assessment, and instruction. The learning experienced by students is more easily measured. Both types of learning, however, are worth it.

References

Ainsworth, L. (2007). Common formative assessments: The centerpiece of an integrated standards-based assessment system. In D. Reeves (Ed.), *Ahead of the curve: The power of assessment to transform teaching and learning* (pp. 79–99). Bloomington, IN: Solution Tree.

Ainsworth, L., & Viegut, D. (2006). *Common formative assessments: How to connect standards-based instruction and assessment*. Thousand Oaks, CA: Corwin.

Black, P., & Wiliam, D. (1998). Assessment and classroom learning. *Assessment in Education, 5*(1), 7–75.

DuFour, R., DuFour, R., & Eaker, R. (2008). *Revisiting professional learning communities at work: New insights for improving schools*. Bloomington, IN: Solution Tree.

Earl, L., & LeMahieu, P. (1997). Rethinking assessment and accountability. In A. Hargreaves (Ed.), *Rethinking educational change with heart and mind* (pp. 149–168). Alexandria, VA: Association for Supervision and Curriculum Development.

Marzano, R. J. (2006). *Classroom assessment and grading that work.* Alexandria, VA: Association for Supervision and Curriculum Development.

Reeves, D. (2002). *The leader's guide to standards: A blueprint for educational equity and excellence.* San Francisco: John Wiley & Sons.

Reeves, D. (2006). *The learning leader.* Alexandria, VA: Association for Supervision and Curriculum Development.

Schmoker, M. (2004). Start here for improving teaching and learning. *School Administrator, 61*(10), 48–49.

Schmoker, M. (2006). *Results now.* Alexandria, VA: Association for Supervision and Curriculum Development.

Stiggins, R. J. (2005). Assessment *for* learning: Building a culture of confident learners. In R. DuFour, R. Eaker, & R. DuFour (Eds.), *On common ground: The power of professional learning communities* (pp. 65–83). Bloomington, IN: Solution Tree (formerly National Educational Service).

Stiggins, R. J., Arter, J. A., Chappuis, J., & Chappuis, S. (2004). *Classroom assessment for student learning: Doing it right—Using it well.* Portland, OR: ETS Assessment Training Institute.

AINSLEY B. ROSE

Ainsley Rose is the former director of education, curriculum, and technology for the Western Quebec School Board in Gatineau, Quebec. As an education leader, he incorporates his expertise in a wide range of principles, practices, and concepts that have been proven to improve schools, including Effective Schools, Professional Learning Communities at Work™, instructional intelligence, and standards and assessment. He also conducts peer mediation for schools and has presented at the International Effective Schools Conference. Ainsley has experience as an elementary and secondary classroom teacher and principal, as well as an instructor of graduate-level courses for administrators and pre-service teachers and presently acts as a senior leadership coach. He has served as chair of the Committee for Anglophone Curriculum Responsables and the Implementation Design Committee, and was named to the Advisory Board on English Education by the Minister of Education of Quebec. Ainsley has also received the Outstanding Achievement Award from the Association of Administrators of English Schools of Quebec. He is a contributor to *The Principal as Assessment Leader* (Solution Tree, 2009) and *The Collaborative Teacher: Working Together as a Professional Learning Community* (Solution Tree, 2008).

SEVEN

Creating Equity in Classroom Assessment for English Language Learners and Students With Special Needs

Ainsley B. Rose

As our nation's rapidly changing demographics make classrooms a meeting place for multiple cultures, the important and difficult task of improving literacy learning for all *children becomes an increasingly complex challenge. Teachers are called on to find ways of ensuring that children from a diversity of backgrounds are able to achieve the same high standards. Meeting this challenge requires that teachers not only understand their students' vastly different experiences and understanding, but also be able to use this knowledge to provide educational experiences responsive to diverse needs.*

—Beverly Falk

The abundance of research on assessment and evaluation reveals that when it comes to grading and reporting for students with special needs, English language learners (ELLs), or gifted and talented students, teachers face many new and unique challenges (Guskey & Bailey, 2001). For example, how do we keep from discouraging learners with special needs while at the same time reporting the truth about their progress or lack of it (Tomlinson & McTighe, 2006)? If we are expected to differentiate instruction, how will we differentiate assessment and evaluation without compromising the principles of authentic, valid, high-quality assessment and evaluation? Grading expert Ken O'Connor (2007) encourages us to carefully consider what constitutes a final grade. For students with special needs who are following programs that may have been adapted or modified, achievement may not always be evident, but a student may exert remarkable effort to produce a piece of work. To what extent should the teacher give additional credit to that student over another who is far more capable but displays little effort in his or her work? What about the impact of the grading process on the motivation of the struggling learner or, for that matter, of the gifted student who has never had to struggle to achieve a "good mark" but always achieves one that is far below what he or she is truly capable of achieving?

This chapter will offer some alternative assessment perspectives for the classroom teacher to consider, while maintaining the integrity of assessment principles and sound instructional practices. We will explore the specific challenges of *grading* in the context of assessing, evaluating, and reporting learning and achievement for English language learners as well as those in bilingual educational programs, students with special needs, and gifted and talented students. All these students deserve particular attention. First, we have to learn so much about how to deal with these students from an instructional perspective, given that school policies at the state or provincial level require adaptation, accommodations, or modification (many jurisdictions consider the latter two terms to be forms of the first) of curriculum and instruction in order to meet their needs. Second, we must ask ourselves, What are the instructional methods that have the greatest impact on their learning? While these questions deal with instruction, we know that instruction is informed by assessment and evaluation. Therefore, the examination of grading and evaluation practices for these students surely needs to be treated with the same reverence afforded our understanding of the instructional process. The old adage "Fair does not mean equal" holds true for assessing and grading (O'Connor, 2007). We must ensure that we use valid and reliable methods that accurately reflect, for each and every learner, our programs and expectations. While I speak of each and every learner, I hasten to add that this chapter will deal primarily with those students with special needs who are integrated into the regular classroom, as opposed to those students with special needs who are simply "included" in regular classrooms. This distinction will be discussed more fully later on.

Understanding Our Students

English Language Learners

Before we go further, we need to understand the students we will be discussing. *English language learners* are students whose first language is not English or who are in the early stages of learning English as the subject in which they are being taught (Sampson, 2009). Lisa Almeida (2007) points out that they have also been referred to as limited English proficiency students (LEPs). Second language learners are students whose mother tongue is not the language of instruction; therefore, they may also be considered ELL or LEP students. Both present similar challenges for assessment, evaluation, and reporting for the classroom teacher. Beyond these students, there are those who spend various amounts of time in bilingual programs where instruction is not conducted in their mother tongue. We would know this more commonly as *second language immersion*. For the purpose of this chapter, the term *English language learner* will be used to represent all of these learners.

Almeida (2007) proposes that we need to consider three essential questions in examining the assessment approaches for English language learners:

1. What do educators need to consider when preparing to meet the assessment needs of English language learners?

2. How can teachers effectively assess English language learners' learning as opposed to their ability to speak the language?

3. What are the roles of teachers and school leaders in creating and sustaining effective assessment opportunities for English language learners? What are our responsibilities as drivers of the education process? (2007, p. 149)

I suggest that these questions can serve for all of the students we will discuss.

Students With Special Needs

Most of us already have a clear notion of students with special needs as those who experience deficits in learning that are usually a result of a learning delay, organic dysfunction, or some other pervasive disorder such as behavior dysfunction or socioemotional maladjustment. In this chapter, *students with special needs* also refers to those students with deafness, blindness, speech aphasia, or similar conditions that prevent them from learning in an inclusive classroom without some form of human, physical, or technological support.

Gifted and Talented Students

Too often, we forget the other end of the spectrum of special needs: students who have been identified as gifted and talented learners also require particular attention. They often go unnoticed but do present similar challenges when it comes to assessment and evaluation.

Understanding Key Terms

We must also define the essential terms of reference that shape this chapter. *Fair, equal,* and *equitable* have significant differences in meaning. *Fair* does not mean *equal; equitable* does not mean *fair.* Dennis Munc (2007) can help to make the distinctions clearer:

A fair grading system:

- Provides an opportunity for high grades to be earned

- Provides meaningful grades that reflect a student's experience in the classroom

- Includes flexibility as needed to meet individual needs of students

An equitable grading system:

- Maintains high student accountability even when a grading system is individualized

- Accurately matches grades to performance, even when accommodations are implemented

What is fair is not always equal. If a teacher has a student in her class who is not able to see the board and therefore moves the student closer to the front of the class, she is making accommodations for that student so that the student has a fair chance at success. Clearly, she can't move all the students to the front, so the situation cannot be equal. *Fair* means to have the same rights, status, and opportunities. *Equitable,* on the other hand, means that students must be treated impartially and fairly. In order to be equitable to all students, we must make accommodations to give students with special needs equal access to success as their classmates.

When we say that *equity* means the quality of being "fair and impartial," we might think we are talking about being fair and impartial to the English language learner and the student with special needs, but true equity requires that we consider all students, including those without special needs or learning obstacles. Lee Ann Jung (2009) points out that we must weigh the approaches when we have a student who is unable to reach proficiency on a standard in a given subject but who surpasses the expectation of his or her IEP (individualized education plan) goals, or a student with several disabilities who is not able to achieve at level but tries very hard and is very conscientious in every respect. Can we really assign a grade using a single grading scale that fairly and impartially reflects both of these cases? If we use different scales, what is the effect on the student without any of the learning obstacles or the student with special needs or the English language learner? This is but one of the many challenges facing teachers with increasing numbers of ELLs and students with special needs in inclusive classrooms (Jung, 2009).

Many students who struggle in their learning are not categorized as students with special needs. We have to ask that if they require extra time and support from the teacher, should we then mark them differently from those who do not require this additional occasional support when learning new material?

As recently as 2004, federal legislation in the United States created the Individuals with Disabilities Education Improvement Act, which essentially outlined what measures schools need to take to ensure that all students become successful regardless of who intervenes to support their learning needs (Buffum, Mattos, & Weber, 2009). *Response to intervention* (RTI), as it is known, "shifts the responsibility for helping students become successful from the special education teachers and curriculum to the entire staff, including special and regular education teachers and curriculum" (p. 2). Of particular note, RTI places increased emphasis on progress monitoring at more frequent intervals. When it comes to grading, author-educators Austin Buffum, Mike Mattos, and Chris Weber suggest that "current grading practices are designed to sort and rank student achievement; they require students who learn quickly and accurately and punish those who require additional time and opportunities to master material" (2009, p. 140).

The many immigrant students who populate our classrooms these days are another group who may require additional help at times. These students may not have been exposed to certain cultural aspects of our curriculum. However, some of these students function at high levels of achievement despite lacking background knowledge of their new culture (Marzano, 2004). Do we give immigrant students special accommodations or make sure we create assessments that are not biased culturally? (Kusimo, Ritter, Busick, & Ferguson, 2000; Stiggins, Arter, Chappuis, & Chappuis, 2004). Of course we do—without hesitation—but do we evaluate and assess these students in the same way? If we expect teachers to differentiate instruction, surely we need to find the means to differentiate assessment and evaluation.

The term *differentiated instruction* has been in vogue to identify the approach that best responds to teaching all students. Rick Wormeli (2006) defines it this way:

> Differentiated instruction is doing what's fair for students. It's a collection of best practices strategically employed to maximize students' learning at every turn, including giving them the tools to handle anything that is undifferentiated. (p. 3)

Remediation, adaptation, modification, and *accommodation* all describe the valiant attempts to differentiate instruction for the students who are the focus of this chapter. In our well-intentioned enthusiasm to meet the instructional needs of these students, we have spawned polices that speak of integration and inclusion synonymously. I contend that to integrate requires the teacher to plan lessons that actually require the student with special needs to actively participate in the learning. Inclusion, on the other hand, simply requires the students be placed physically in a regular classroom without any real expectation that the student will be participating intellectually in what the rest of the class is learning. Thomas Guskey and Jane Bailey (2001) report U.S. Department of Education findings that in U.S. schools, "80% of students with disabilities spend the major portion of their school day in general education classes" (p. 109). While this statistic is interesting, it does not in itself explain the learning expectations for these students. Are they simply being included, or is this a real attempt to integrate them into the learning? The distinction is important, as it makes a huge difference when we seek to assess the learning of those students. While educators make commendable attempts to meet the needs of a hard-to-serve population in schools, we come up short in the assessment, evaluation, and reporting of their achievement; we have different expectations of students in inclusive classrooms but do not necessarily have different means to assess them.

As with many of our approaches in teaching and learning, we tend to use a norm to categorize students—"the average." Students who do not fit the image of the "average" student require some sort of "special" treatment. "Regular" students get "regular" programs and "regular" teachers in "regular" classrooms. Those who don't fit the norm are categorized after some identification or testing process—grouped and sorted into programs that are intended to remediate their inabilities and shortcomings or enrich their advantages in learning as compared to regular students. Gifted and talented students, students with special needs, and English language learners all fit this class of students who do not fit the norm and therefore pose real challenges for teachers and school administrators (Guskey & Bailey, 2001).

Understanding Issues in Grading and Reporting

Grading and reporting practices require careful examination when it comes to instructional methodologies for the students in question. However, let us not forget that the actual act of *taking* the test or exam presents other challenges to the classroom teacher, the student, and the school. Again, one must ask pertinent questions such as, Should students have their conditions for taking a test modified to reflect their instructional program, or is that unfair to other students who may, for example, have timelines imposed by which they need to complete an assignment or test?

English language learners, students with special needs, and gifted and talented students each require different treatment when it comes to addressing their assessment needs. English language learners present particular challenges to the classroom teacher. For example, can the ELL student understand English to the point that he or she can be accurately assessed in the content of a subject? (Kusimo et al., 2000) Teachers could easily conclude that an ELL is not competent because the student's inability to understand the language may hide his or her true understanding of the content.

Students with special needs come in various categories: some are included in the regular classroom, others are placed in self-contained special education classes, and others are integrated and expected to follow the regular curriculum but require accommodations when it comes to testing situations. These categories suggest that different conditions exist that may well lead to different conclusions on the part of classroom teachers as to a student's level of competency on any given task, assignment, or test.

The gifted and talented students by definition have superior skills that are often developed earlier than their peers. Therefore, a high mark (A) could simply reflect knowledge that was acquired two to three years earlier rather than new knowledge acquired in the present grade or course (Guskey & Bailey, 2001).

Grading Philosophies

Guskey and Bailey point out that "although educators generally agree on the need to adapt educational practices for students with disabilities in general education classes, it is evident that these students are relatively unsuccessful when evaluated in terms of traditional grading practices" (2001, p. 111). They suggest four prevailing grading philosophies for children with special needs in inclusive classrooms:

1. Applying the same grading standards to all students

2. Grading in terms of individual effort

3. Grading in terms of learning progress

4. Making specific grading adaptations (2001, p. 110)

Each of these approaches has advantages and disadvantages, although all depend a great deal on the perception and beliefs of individual teachers, as we have seen with other grading policies in different circumstances (Marzano, 2000).

Applying the same grading standards to all students, the first philosophy, means that regardless of a student's disabilities or accommodations, if he or she receives a particular mark, it should mean the same achievement as it does for all students. This approach clearly puts students with learning disabilities at a huge disadvantage because most are not able to achieve at a higher level than where they already are (Guskey & Bailey, 2001). Yet this remains a common philosophy in some jurisdictions to marking children with special needs, given that many educators believe that there should be no lowering of expectations for students taking the same course or program.

The second philosophy, grading in terms of individual effort, suggests that grades should reflect the particular effort a student puts into his or her learning. If students with special needs have made great efforts to overcome their shortcomings as learners, this should be reflected in their marks. This is best accomplished by reporting a separate mark for achievement distinct from effort. But how is a teacher to know whether a given student's performance reflects his or her best effort?

According to the third philosophy, students with special needs should be graded based on progress over time, such as a term or semester. We often have heard it said, "Begin where students are, and take them as far as a teacher can from there." The challenge here is for schools and teachers in particular to ensure that performance criteria, benchmarks, and indicators are clearly outlined and depicted as graduated levels of performance along a continuum from novice to proficient to advanced. While there may be some who would argue that students with special needs will never achieve proficient or advanced levels of performance, it is incumbent that the expectations represented by the graduated levels be made clear for all students. We must always expect that *all* students will strive for improved performance, and therefore students need to see what the expectations are for higher levels and quality of work. This gives the students and their parents a clear picture of progress as goals to be achieved. The difficulty with this approach is summed up by Guskey and Bailey (2001), who imagine a student saying, "The best thing about my individualized instructional program is that I am falling behind at my own pace" (p. 114).

The fourth approach is illustrated by table 7.1 (page 166), which presents three methods of grading adaptations available to teachers with students with special needs. Method 1 uses changes in criteria to determine a grade, whereas method 2 allows for the use of supplemental information to determine the grade. Method 3 provides the options of using checklists of skills to track mastery or using a pass/fail system (Guskey & Bailey, 2001). These suggestions reinforce the notion of differentiation when speaking about instruction for students with special needs. If we expect teachers to differentiate instruction, then it is implicit that we expect teachers to differentiate assessment and grading as well. Teachers can apply these suggestions judiciously as needed. It might help us to remember that grades serve several purposes. Stiggins, Arter, Chappuis, and Chappuis

Table 7.1: Common Grading Adaptations for Students With Disabilities

Adaptation	Example
Change Grading Criteria	
Vary grading weights assigned to different activities and/or products.	Increase credit for participation in classroom group activities and decrease credit for essay examinations. (Note: We now know this is problematic in a standards-based environment.)
Grade on improvement by assigning extra points.	Change a *C* to a *B* if the student's total points have increased significantly from the previous marking period. (Note: This doesn't work if the student's grade is to reflect the current level of achievement.)
Modify or individualize curriculum expectations.	Indicate in the IEP that the student will work on subtraction while the other students work on division.
Use contracts and modified course requirements for quality, quantity, and timelines.	State in the contract that the student will receive a *B* for completing all assignments at 80% quantity and timelines, accuracy, attending all classes, and completing one extra-credit report.
Provide Supplemental Information	
Add written comments to clarify details about the criteria used.	Write on the report card that the student's grade represents performance on the IEP objectives and not on the regular curriculum.
Add information from the student activity log.	Note that while the student's grade was the same this marking period, daily records show the student completed math assignments with less teacher assistance.
Add information about effort, progress, and achievement from portfolios or performance-based assignments.	State that the student's written language showed an increase in word variety, sentence length, and quality of ideas.
Use Other Grading Options	
Use checklists of skills and show the number or percentage of objectives met.	Attach a checklist to the report card indicating that during the marking period, the student mastered addition facts, two-digit addition with regrouping, and counting change to one dollar.
Use pass/fail grades.	Students receive a "pass" for completing 80% of daily work with at least 70% accuracy, and attending 90% of class sessions.

Source: *Developing Grading and Reporting Systems for Student Learning* (p. 118), by Thomas Guskey and Jane Bailey. Copyright 2000 by Sage Publications Inc. Books. Reproduced with permission of Sage Publications Inc. Books in the format Other book via Copyright Clearance Center.

(2004) point out that grades should first communicate; they should communicate about achievement primarily; and they should reflect the most recent level of achievement in order to portray an accurate picture of student learning.

These four approaches provide some hope of a solution if the method chosen can be distinguished from the others so that marks on a report card are clear, truthful, and, if possible, positive. Parents make judgments about their child's progress on the basis of the report cards and test results they see throughout the school year. Consider, for example, the conclusions parents of children with special needs may come to if they continually receive reports that their child is performing at high levels relative to his or her IEP goals or expectations; they might conclude that their child no longer requires special services. Conversely, low marks would suggest that their child is not making appropriate progress and that there was something wrong with the instruction or the service to which their child was entitled.

How do we deal with the challenge of either giving a passing grade to an English language learner or a student with special needs who has not met the standards, or failing a student who has made valiant effort and progress toward his or her IEP goals? Can we reconcile both these in a normal testing situation and expect to have clarity of purpose when reporting achievement to students and their parents? In addition, students with special needs and English language learners often have more than one teacher who is responsible for their learning. What degree of responsibility for the final grade does a teacher have for the student who attends her class for part of a course or program, but receives the rest of his instruction in a self-contained classroom? Many such students have teacher aides present in the classroom; does the aide have input into the final grades of those children?

Invariably, there are more questions than answers. Many schools do not have clear policies, resulting in unfair grading and reporting practices that affect all students, not just those identified as requiring special considerations. There must be equity in approach and purpose, but as the title of Rick Wormeli's 2006 book states, fair isn't always equal.

Differentiated Instruction and Assessment

Wormeli (2005) states the following in an article on ten myths about differentiated education:

> First, differentiated instruction and standardized tests are not oxymoronic. Some principals think that if teachers differentiate in their classes, students will be disabled when they take state assessments that are not differentiated. Nothing could be farther from the truth. Students will do well on standardized assessments if they know the material well, and differentiated instruction's bottom line is to teach in whatever way students best learn. (p. 1)

This supports the notion that when grading students—regardless of their disability or lack thereof—and reporting their grades, we must not compare students against *one another*; rather, we must compare their achievement *against the standard to which we are teaching* (Marzano, 2000). Therefore, progress is an important consideration when grading *all* students. English language learners, gifted and talented students, and students with special needs can be seen as progressing rather than failing even if they are not at the same level or in the same program as other students in the class. To put it simply, students' grades should be based on the extent to which they progress beyond their initial learning or understanding of a topic. The challenge we have is to communicate that appropriately to parents and students without disadvantaging any other student.

To understand what criteria we use to measure progress, it may help to explain the differences among product, process, and progress goals. For a product goal, we consider first and foremost what students know and can do at a specific time, usually at the end of a reporting period or learning sequence.

Teachers who believe that there is more to learning than just the final product—that how students got to where they are reveals a great deal about their learning and should be reflected in their marks—use process criteria. They consider class participation, homework, and attendance in calculating grades.

Teachers who believe that growth over time truly reflects what students have gained from their learning use progress criteria. Students who began with a grade of C and progressed to a B show growth that needs to be documented and recognized (Guskey & Bailey, 2001). Progress criteria differ from product criteria in that the teacher considers the extent of improvement the student has made on a variety of assessments, including assessments *for* learning. When using product criteria, the teacher takes into account only one measure of student learning at a specific point in time. This assessment *of* learning does not consider where the student was when he or she first began the learning that was the focus of the assessment.

Accommodations

In responding to the needs of the students we have been discussing, we must take into account that most provinces and states have procedures if not requirements for schools and districts to offer either modifications or accommodations to students who have been formally categorized as requiring special services (Sampson, 2009; Guskey & Bailey, 2001). Shannon Sampson references the work of Tindal, Hollenbeck, Heath, and Almond (1997) to define the two terms *modifications* and *accommodations:*

Accommodations do not change the nature of the construct being tested, but rather provide access to the test. Modifications, on the other hand, change the test. . . . An accommodation is an adjustment to how a student accesses information and demonstrates understanding. A modification is an adjustment to what educators expect a student to learn, so the goal itself is modified. (Sampson, 2009, p. 43)

Some accommodations will depend to a large extent on the student's disability or program (ELL, gifted and talented, and so on). These accommodations may include extra time to complete an exam, the use of a glossary of English terms, or access to a scribe, as long as the use of such accommodations does not give the student any advantage over others who do not have those resources available to them in taking the test. The accommodations selected must be those that would most benefit the student; they are not equally useful. Accommodations that may not be appropriate for English language learners might be most helpful to a child with special needs.

Modifications, on the other hand, might include changing the instructional level expectations for students. For example, a grade 5 student with severe disabilities in mathematics who is not able to demonstrate computational skills in fractions and decimals—a common instructional goal in grade 5—may be learning addition and subtraction facts at the grade 3 level and would be assessed on his or her ability to meet the grade 3 level expectations. Similarly, gifted and talented students may need work or assessments at a grade or so above their present placement in order to challenge them more appropriately. An ELL student with limited reading ability might be given leveled reading material rather than the novel other students in that grade may be studying.

It is important to note, however, that in the United States, since No Child Left Behind, this meaning of the term *modifications* on state testing for students with disabilities has been replaced with *alternative assessments based on alternate academic content standards*: "an alternate achievement standard is an expectation of performance that differs in complexity from a grade-level achievement standard. The availability of this type of assessment has been established for a very small percentage of students with disabilities who cannot participate in the state's assessment program even with accommodations" (Cortiella, 2004).

(For a more complete examination of the complexities and shortcomings in making accommodations and modifications, see the interesting work of Kusimo, Ritter, Busick, & Ferguson, 2000.)

Recommendations and Conclusions

Solutions to the dilemmas presented in this chapter are not as evident as we might hope. Many experts and researchers do not agree on the best methods to assess, evaluate, and report learning for these students. Sampson (2009) cites the work of Guskey and Bailey as well as of Rick Stiggins; they all appear to share the most common approach. They propose that we need to gather evidence of learning in each of the product, process, and progress areas in a *standards-based system of assessment*. This approach allows the most flexibility for teachers to adapt or modify their instruction in classes with English language learners, students with special needs, and gifted students—even if those students attend for only part of their instruction. Other methods present too many restrictions to allow teachers to get accurate, valid, and reliable measures of progress over time. Standards-based reporting still does not eliminate the known discrepancies in assessment and evaluation that have been documented by many researchers in like subjects, like grades, and like schools (Guskey & Bailey, 2001). These discrepancies include bias and distortion in some testing instruments as well as differences in teacher professional judgment, grading and reporting practices (even with guides), benchmark descriptors for proficiency for a course or a grade, and selection of appropriate assessment tools for the knowledge being assessed (Stiggins et al., 2004). We also know that the same work marked by different teachers can have variance of two or more grade levels depending on the perspective of those teachers (Marzano, 2006). This should tell us that we need to be judicious about whatever methods we use, as much can go wrong even when well intentioned and well informed.

A Reality Check

Though assessing product, process, and progress is indeed an appropriate method, we must question whether we can assess all of these equally in the different groups identified in this chapter. While the need to test and report each of these indicators is important in our grading practices, the bigger issue is to ensure that process and progress scores (or indicators, or grades) are distinct from the product or achievement grade. This is a complex task; the classroom teacher still bears great responsibility to make sense of these factors before rendering a sound professional judgment about any one of them. Consider an elementary teacher in an urban school with a somewhat transient population. Of the twenty-five students in her class, six are identified as having special needs, two are high achievers or possibly gifted, and two others moved into her class six weeks after the beginning of the new term. One of those new students has limited English skills; his parents speak no English at all.

Teachers in schools across North America find themselves in quite similar positions. Once we can accept that this is now a common occurrence, we must evaluate what learning decisions, instructional strategies, and assessment and evaluation considerations this teacher must craft in order to feel she is meeting the instructional needs of her students. How will she begin to create appropriate learning situations for her students and then make a professional judgment for a report card that may or may not be understood by the parents of her students, let alone the students themselves?

Secondary or middle school teachers are often required to teach upwards of 100 to 150 students in the course of their workweek. This volume must have an impact on teachers' ability to make sound pedagogical decisions while taking into account differentiation of instruction and accommodations and modifications for students who require them or who by law are entitled to specialized programs. Students' individualized education programs have identified what their teachers must ensure they learn—or face sanction or possible censure from school districts and other agencies or, worse, the wrath of parents who rightfully advocate for their children. How can we give teachers a reasonable chance to respond adequately to the needs of these students without disadvantaging the other, often forgotten students? We must not create another class of disadvantaged students where none existed previously.

A Model for Meeting Student Needs

The truth is, we adapt testing procedures for students who have observable disabilities such as blindness or deafness, and we don't consider those special considerations "unfair." There is no reason why we can't give students with special needs and English language learners similar accommodations.

Jung & Guskey (2007) provide a model to help teachers think through what should be considered when making instructional and assessment decisions for special categories of students. The five steps of their model are:

1. Determine if any accommodations or modifications are needed for each grade-level standard,

2. Establish the appropriate modified standard for each area requiring modification,

3. Outline additional goals pertinent to the child's academic success,

4. Apply equal grading practices to the appropriate standards, and

5. Clearly communicate the meaning of grades. (p. 31)

Applying equal grading practices means that once a school or district has clearly identified purpose, product, and progress separately, it remains for the teacher to apply those practices for different categories of students with special needs—indeed, ELLs and gifted and talented students as well. In other words, as Jung (2009) says, "With questions on *what* and *how* to grade answered, adaptations to the grading process are no longer needed" (p. 34). If a school district does not have clear guidelines about purpose, product, and progress identified separately for all teachers, then it is left to the devices of individual teachers—which then results in the reporting inaccuracies that we presently see. If the guidelines are clear, there is no need to adapt the grading any longer because the product, process, and purpose are reported differently for all students, making it fair for everyone. The strategies in table 7.1 (page 166) help create a systems approach in the absence of other guidelines.

A grade often tries to communicate many different things to parents and students. What is required is clear and accurate information about product, process, and progress. Guskey (2009) writes:

> Providing grades that are based on modified standards without communicating what was truly measured is not more meaningful or fair than giving failing grades based on grade-level standards. If some or all of the grades for achievement are based on modified standards, then the reporting system must include additional information to ensure that families understand their child's success is based on work appropriate for their development level instead of their assigned grade level. (p. 34)

For a more thorough understanding of this model, the reader is encouraged to read the full account.

A Change of Heart

Another point that warrants examination is the extent to which we have developed unhelpful habits as a result of our collective preoccupation in labeling students with deficits. Beverly Falk (1998) points out that "as teachers recognize the varying [strengths] of diverse learners, they become less likely to attach labels to children (e.g., José is a troublemaker) or to make all-inclusive judgments about them (Shanta can't read)" (p. 50).

As educators, we need to take a strengths-based approach. We should not assume that an English language learner does not have the potential to learn at high levels. Far too much is made of what students are not able to do. As a result, we do not hold high expectations for these students, and invariably, our low expectations are met. Falk (1998) reminds us:

> These labels have the unintended effect of becoming self-fulfilling prophecies. The child for whom adults have low expectations dutifully produces what is expected: the child who is labeled with a particular problem conforms to that image held by others. As a result, teachers and schools often inadvertently set limits on the learning opportunities for these students. Although the intent may be to provide appropriate settings for students with special problems, the actual effect is to deny students access to challenging curriculum. This, in turn, constrains their abilities to develop intellectual rigor and to achieve high standards. (p. 50)

Another intervention that has shown great promise is the Primary Language Record, a process described by Falk (1998) as having great potential to remediate and reduce significantly the deficits of English language learners and students with special needs. The process asks teachers to collect and reflect on concrete evidence about their students (both those with special considerations and those with none)—to record their learning tendencies and habits in order to appreciate the many ways that students learn, despite being identified in a given category.

The urgency to meet the learning, assessment, and reporting needs of our students is escalating. The number of students is increasing, and so is our frustration as educators that we're not meeting our students' needs adequately (Kusimo, Ritter, Busick, & Ferguson, 2000; Marzano, 2003). Yes, we need to acquaint ourselves with the various policies and processes, but with the conviction that fair does not mean equal. With continued support and increasing assessment literacy, we will develop a more informed educational community that embraces the challenge to provide for all learners using a balanced, equitable approach.

References and Resources

Allen, D. (Ed.). (1998). *Assessing student learning: From grading to understanding*. New York: Teachers College.

Almeida, L. (2007). The journey toward effective assessment for English language learners. In D. Reeves (Ed.), *Ahead of the curve: The power of assessment to transform teaching and learning* (pp. 147–163). Bloomington, IN: Solution Tree.

Buffum, A., Mattos, M., & Weber, C. (2009). *Pyramid response to intervention: RTI, professional learning communities, and how to respond when kids don't learn*. Bloomington, IN: Solution Tree.

Cortiella, C. (2004, March). *Accommodations, modifications, and alternative assessments: How they affect instruction and assessment*. Accessed at www.greatschools.net/cgi-bin/showarticle/2786 on May 27, 2009.

Falk, B. (1998). Looking at students and their work: Supporting diverse learners with the primary language record. In D. Allen (Ed.), *Assessing student learning: From grading to understanding* (pp. 40–65). New York: Teachers College.

Guskey, T. R. (Ed.). (2009). *Practical solutions for serious problems in standards-based grading*. Thousand Oaks, CA: Corwin.

Guskey, T. R., & Bailey, J. M. (2001). *Developing grading and reporting systems for student learning*. Thousand Oaks, CA: Corwin.

Guskey, T. R., & Jung, L. A. (2006, Winter). The challenges of standards-based grading. *Leadership Compass, 4*(2). Accessed at www.naesp. org/resources/2/Leadership_Compass/2006/LC2006v4n2a3.pdf on November 19, 2008.

Jung, L. A. (2009). The challenges of grading and reporting in special education: An inclusive grading model. In T. R. Guskey (Ed.), *Practical solutions for serious problems in standards-based grading* (pp. 27–40). Thousand Oaks, CA: Corwin.

Jung, L. A., & Guskey, T. R. (2007). Standards-based grading and reporting: A model for special education. *Teaching Exceptional Children, 40*(2), 48–53.

Kusimo, P., Ritter, M., Busick, K., & Ferguson, C. (2000). *Making assessment work for everyone: How to build on student strengths.* Assessment Laboratory Network Project of the Regional Educational Laboratories. San Francisco: WestEd.

Marzano, R. (2000). *Transforming classroom grading.* Alexandria, VA: Association for Supervision and Curriculum Development.

Marzano, R. (2003). *What works in schools: Translating research into action.* Alexandria, VA: Association for Supervision and Curriculum Development.

Marzano, R. (2004). *Building background knowledge for academic achievement: Research on what works in schools.* Alexandria, VA: Association for Supervision and Curriculum Development.

Marzano, R. (2006). *Classroom assessment and grading that work.* Alexandria, VA: Association for Supervision and Curriculum Development.

Munc, D. (2007, October). *Fair and equitable grading practices for students with LD who have IEPs.* Accessed at www.greatschools.net/cgi-bin/showarticle/3154 on November 19, 2008.

National Center on Educational Outcomes. (2008, September). *Middle school principals' perspectives on academic standards-based instruction and programming for English language learners with disabilities.* Accessed at http://cehd.umn.edu/NCEO/OnlinePubs/ELLsDis22/ELLsDisRpt22.pdf on November 3, 2008.

O'Connor, K. (2007). *A repair kit for grading: 15 fixes for broken grades.* Portland, OR: Educational Testing Service.

Popham, J. (2003). *Test better, teach better: The instructional role of assessment.* Alexandria, VA: Association for Supervision and Curriculum Development.

Reeves, D. (2003). *Making standards work: How to implement standards-based assessments in the classroom, school, and district.* Englewood, CO: Advanced Learning.

Reeves, D. (Ed.). (2007). *Ahead of the curve: The power of assessment to transform teaching and learning.* Bloomington, IN: Solution Tree.

Sampson, S. O. (2009). Assigning fair, accurate, and meaningful grades to students who are English language learners. In T. R. Guskey (Ed.), *Practical solutions for serious problems in standards-based grading* (pp. 41–56). Thousand Oaks, CA: Corwin.

Stiggins, R. J., Arter, J. A., Chappuis, J, & Chappuis, S. (2004). *Classroom assessment for student learning: Doing it right—Using it well.* Portland, OR: ETS Assessment Training Institute.

Tomlinson, C. A., & McTighe, J. (2006). *Integrating differentiated instruction and Understanding by Design: Connecting content and kids.* Alexandria, VA: Association for Supervision and Curriculum Development.

Wormeli, R. (2005, March). Busting myths about differentiated instruction. *Principal Leadership.* Accessed at www.wilmette39.org/DI39/dipdf/BustingMythsaboutDI.pdf on November 3, 2008.

Wormeli, R. (2006). *Fair isn't always equal: Assessing and grading in the differentiated classroom.* Portland, ME: Stenhouse.

PART THREE

Involving Students in Assessment

JEFFRY OVERLIE

Jeffry Overlie is the International Baccalaureate Primary Years Programme coordinator for Fridley Public Schools in Fridley, Minnesota. In addition to providing leadership for the implementation of this program, Jeff is responsible for overseeing curriculum development and standard articulation and providing professional development at the elementary level. Jeffry also works as an adjunct professor of education at Bethel University in St. Paul, Minnesota, where he participated on the program design team to write a Master's level certificate program in International Baccalaureate Education. He has fifteen years of classroom and leadership experience that span elementary, middle, and high school levels. During his time in the classroom, Jeff has taught in self-contained, departmentalized, and multiage classrooms as well as in team teaching situations. He earned his Master of Arts in education from Hamline University.

EIGHT

Creating Confident, Capable Learners

Jeffry Overlie

In talking with teachers about classroom practice, I have rarely encountered an individual who is opposed to involving students in learning activities. Although many teachers still employ the old sit-and-get philosophy of delivering information to students, it is gradually becoming just one strategy among several. When I stress the importance of involving students in the *assessment* process, however, I often encounter more skepticism, disbelief, or opposition.

I often hear comments such as "With everything I am expected to teach, I do not have time to involve students in assessment," or "I have tried involving students in the assessment process, but all students do not take it seriously, so it is a waste of time," or "My students lack the skills to follow through when given some of the responsibility in their assessment." I empathize with statements such as these, but I believe they are often made by teachers who have not fully explored how to effectively involve students in the assessment process. This chapter presents research that shows why involving students in their assessment needs to become the rule rather than the exception and provides self-assessment models that could transfer to any K–12 classroom as a means to involve students in the assessment process.

The Importance of Involving Students in Assessment

In *Classroom Assessment* for *Student Learning: Doing It Right—Using It Well* (2004), Rick Stiggins, Judith Arter, Jan Chappuis, and Stephen Chappuis articulate the importance of involving students in the assessment process. Because students are ultimately responsible for making decisions regarding their education, they must play a key role in all aspects of their education, including assessment. For example, a student who clearly understands the intended learning targets can more easily analyze his or her assessment results to determine what to focus on improving. Student involvement through formative assessment, and in particular self-assessment, engages students as active participants in the education process.

The Research: Formative Assessment

In looking at the benefits of involving students in their assessment, we must first look at the research supporting the use of formative assessment. In high-quality formative assessment, students become partners with teachers. Traditionally, many teachers have seen assessment as a means to motivate students, believing that an assessment will push students to perform up to expectations. Stiggins (2005) goes as far as saying that assessment is the "great intimidator," putting demands on students in order to produce greater effort (p. 234). Under this belief, the pressure of assessment causes more learning to take place.

Some students thrive in this environment. From the earliest grades, they learn quickly, score high on assessments, and see themselves as capable learners. Therefore, these students grow confident, are willing to take risks, and always see success within their reach. Unfortunately, this is not the case with all students. As other students score low on assessments, they see themselves as unsuccessful and lose confidence. They feel embarrassed, and their motivation decreases. As these students get older and further behind, they may eventually stop trying. Those students who drop out or who are in the bottom one-third to one-half of the rank order fail to develop the essential reading, writing, and math skills necessary to be successful in our increasingly complex and diverse culture (Stiggins, 2005).

In the days when the school's responsibility was to rank and order students according to their abilities, a lack of motivation was seen as the student's problem rather than the school's problem. Today, however, when all students are expected to meet minimum standards, this belief can no longer be accepted (Stiggins, 2005). Schools need to revise assessment and grading procedures to provide a learning environment that allows all students to see themselves as competent, capable learners. Teachers must believe that all students can achieve a certain level of academic success, and they must make the students believe that as well. All students need to believe that success is within their reach (Stiggins, 2005). The driving forces of this environment must be confidence, optimism, and persistence for all students. Formative assessment, if used correctly, triggers an optimistic response to assessment results by all learners (Stiggins, 2005). This, I believe, can increase student motivation.

There is ample research that suggests that involving students in the assessment process through implementing high-quality formative assessment strategies has a positive impact on student achievement. In *Formative Assessment: Raising Standards Inside the Classroom*, Paul Black (1998) draws on his extensive review of the research evidence on formative assessment to show its effect on student achievement. All of the studies he reviewed produced significant learning gains; the typical standard deviation effect size was between 0.4 and 0.7. According to Black, "an effect size of 0.4 would mean that the average pupil involved in an innovation would record the same achievement as a pupil in the top 35% of those not involved" (1998, p. 141). Reviews of research by Gary Natriello (1987) and Terence Crooks (1988) also show substantial learning gains with the integration of formative assessment strategies into classroom practice.

Dylan Wiliam, Clara Lee, Christine Harrison, and Paul Black (2004) studied the effects of formative assessment on the results of externally mandated assessments, such as national or district tests and examinations. The teachers involved in the study were not given a prescribed model for implementing formative assessment in their classroom. Rather, they were trained on the principles of formative assessment, given time to experiment with the strategies and techniques in their classroom, and asked to create an action plan for implementation in the classroom. These teachers' classrooms were compared to classrooms that were as similar as possible but whose teachers had not received the formative assessment trainings. Most ideally, a comparison was made with a parallel class taught by another teacher during the same year, but when that wasn't an option, the comparison was made in one of two ways: comparing a parallel class of the same teacher from a previous year, or comparing to a nonparallel class taught by the same or a different teacher during the same school year. The results were encouraging, with twenty-one of the twenty-five classrooms whose teachers had received the training posting positive effect sizes. With these results, the authors conclude that if formative assessment were implemented across an entire school whose performance was currently at the 25th percentile, achievement could be raised to above the 50th percentile. Although one needs to be cautious when interpreting these data due to the number of variables involved, Wiliam et al. (2004) believe that their study provides evidence that using formative assessment does produce improved results on externally mandated tests.

A further finding by Black (1998) is that the use of formative assessment greatly improves the achievement of students who have difficulty learning. In a comparison study in which a control group of middle school science classes worked in traditional methods and an experimental group worked with formative assessment, the experimental group improved at a greater rate than the control group. Even more impressive, however, were the findings when the groups were broken down into three groups according to low, medium, and high scores. Those in the low-scoring group surpassed their control-group peers by more than 3 standard deviations. The medium and high experimental groups also showed more improvement than their control-group peers: the medium group just over 2 standard deviations and the high group just over 1 deviation.

The Research: Self-Assessment

Direct research also shows the benefits of self-assessment when isolated from other formative assessment strategies. After surveying students who had engaged in formal self-assessment, Heidi Andrade and Ying Du (2007) found that students felt more prepared, produced higher quality work, and had a clearer understanding of what was expected of them. In addition, these students felt greater motivation and were better at identifying the strengths and weaknesses in their work. Although this research was conducted with university undergraduate students, engaging in self-assessment has also been shown to increase student achievement in the K–12 classroom (Andrade, Du, & Wang, 2007; Lewbel & Hibbard, 2001; Ross, Hogaboam-Gray, & Rolheiser, 2002; White & Frederiksen, 1998) and on external national tests (MacDonald & Boud, 2003).

Siobhan Leahy, Christine Lyon, Marnie Thompson, and Dylan Wiliam (2005) report that, when implementing self-assessment successfully, students take more ownership of their learning, thus making them more effective learners. Black and Wiliam (1998) draw similar conclusions. In addition, they show that participating in self-assessment promotes discussion with others that encourages the reflection on one's own thinking that is essential to good learning. Self-assessment helps students understand what they need to do to achieve.

The Research: The Brain and Thinking

Finally, there is a correlation between brain research, teaching students how to think, and the need to involve students in the assessment process. Starting in the 1990s, there was an explosion of information about how the brain works and the importance of teaching students how to think (Wolfe & Brandt, 1998). This holds implications for educational best practices. One powerful insight is that the brain changes physiologically as a result of experience; thus, providing an enriched environment has a direct impact on the brain's growth and learning (Wolfe & Brandt, 1998). In order to provide this enriched environment for students, teachers need to allow them to be active participants rather than passive observers in their education (Diamond & Hopson, 1998). This gives students the opportunity to make sense out of what they are learning and relate what they are learning to what they already know (Wolfe & Brandt, 1998). Geoffrey Caine, an accomplished author who writes about the influence of brain research on education reform, emphasizes this in an interview with Marcia D'Arcangelo (1998), saying that students need to become more active in their learning. The learning environment needs to move from the old stand-and-deliver model to a partnership between the teacher and the student.

Ron Ritchhart and David Perkins (2008) have conducted research with students from elementary through university settings on the impact of teaching thinking skills and the importance of teaching students to make their thinking visible. They conclude that students' understanding of content increases when they show their thought processes as they work with information through speaking, writing, drawing, or some other method of visualization. Their research also shows an increase in participation and motivation by students.

Shifting From Assessment of Learning to Assessment for Learning

A phrase gaining popularity in education is assessment *for* learning (formative assessment), which implies that students use assessment results to further learning, as opposed to assessment *of* learning (summative assessment), which simply holds students accountable for their learning. Assessment *for* learning is about diagnosing student needs, planning the next steps of instruction, and providing students with the necessary feedback to help facilitate improvement. This kind of assessment helps students feel in control of their journey to success, focuses on improvement (Stiggins et al., 2004), and emphasizes what the students are getting out of the assessment process. In a classroom that uses assessment *for* learning, the separation between instruction and assessment blurs. Everything students do is a potential source of information about how much they understand (Leahy et al., 2005). Assessment *for* learning is not a finite end to learning; it occurs before, during, and after learning.

Assessment *for* learning can be boiled down to students working through three questions, based on the work of Sadler (as analyzed by Stiggins et al., 2004, p. 42):

1. Where am I going? [Students understand the learning targets they are working to master.]

2. Where am I now? [Students understand where their understanding is in relation to mastering the learning target.]

3. How can I close my learning gap? [Students understand what they need to do to improve on learning targets they have not yet mastered.]

Answering these three questions helps ensure that students feel in control of their environment, allowing them to be challenged without being threatened. When assessments directly involve students working to answer these questions, they are assessment *for* learning. In fact, it is not possible to implement assessment *for* learning without direct student involvement.

Meaningful Self-Assessment

There are many important characteristics of assessment *for* learning: providing students with descriptive feedback, engaging students in meaningful classroom discussions, and setting clear learning targets, to name just a few. The most vital component, in my opinion, is engaging students in meaningful self-assessment.

According to Andrade (2008), self-assessment is the process by which students reflect on the quality of their work, based on clearly articulated goals or criteria, and improve their work. It is a form of feedback in which students are in charge of giving and responding to the feedback. Self-assessment is at the heart of everything Stiggins and his colleagues advocate.

The case for helping students become partners in their educational process through self-assessment is compelling, yet I find that teachers often feel intimidated when asked to implement self-assessments. Fortunately, there are some easy ways to begin using self-assessment in your classroom.

Traffic Light Cards

One way to start engaging students in self-assessment is by handing out "traffic light" cards for students to flash to show their level of understanding. Green means the student understands the concept and can explain it, yellow means the student does not understand the concept yet, and red means the student is in need of help.

This concept can be adapted for older students using a medium other than traffic cards. For example, a teacher can teach hand signals to indicate understanding or written symbols to record on individual whiteboards. These methods give the teacher vital information on the understanding of the class as a whole and can be effective in identifying the students in need of remediation. They also help students think about their level of understanding and make judgments that will affect their future instruction.

Journaling

Keeping a journal or blog is another way for students to self-assess. The teacher need only provide an open-ended prompt to start students, such as, What have we concluded? What remains unresolved or unanswered? (Wiggins & McTighe, 2005) In order for this self-assessment strategy to be successful, the teacher must respond to the student's journal or blog. There must be a dialogue in which the instructor gives students guidance about how to close their learning gaps.

Self-Assessments Attached to Summative Assessments

Grant Wiggins and Jay McTighe (2005) also advocate attaching a self-assessment to every formal product or performance. They cite the success of a system at Alverno College in Milwaukee, Wisconsin, which requires a self-assessment after every formal assessment. At Alverno College, all papers must include a self-assessment, and the thoroughness and accuracy of the self-assessment is graded as well as the product. In fact, on some occasions, only the self-assessment and improvement plan are graded.

At the end of any assessment, students could be asked to reflect using questions such as: "Knowing what I do now, what would I do differently next time? What goals do I need to set for myself based on my performance? How well did I do?" Jay McTighe and Ken O'Connor (2005) suggest the following probing questions for students to self-assess, set goals, and plan improvements to work:

- What aspect of your work was most effective?

- What aspect of your work was least effective?

- What specific action or actions will improve your performance?

- What will you do differently next time? (p. 13)

In order for this strategy to be successful, the teacher must ensure that students follow through with an improvement plan.

Pre-Testing

Another approach to helping students self-assess is to assess before teaching. Although teachers have primarily used pretesting as a diagnostic tool to guide their teaching, students can use this information as well. Pre-assessments give students a point of reference of their understanding before learning. Students can later compare their starting points with their summative assessment results to analyze how much their understanding has grown. A simple strategy outlined by Wiggins and McTighe (2005) is to make the first and last assignments of a unit the same. After completion of the last assignment, ask students to write a personal narrative describing their sense of progress in understanding.

Portfolios

Portfolios can also be used to help students assess their growth in understanding. Teachers need to set aside time for students to do a periodic portfolio review and reflect on specific probing questions pertaining to their understanding, such as: "In what ways does your work show your strengths and weaknesses? In what area have you improved the most?"

Differentiating Self-Assessments

All of these strategies are ways to get your students involved in their assessment through self-assessment, and I believe that all of these strategies can have positive results when used correctly. None of them will be the best for every teacher or every student. Using traffic light cards gives great information to a teacher for making teaching decisions, for example, but some students have a difficult time assessing their own level of understanding. With the number of students some teachers see throughout the day, it may be unrealistic to maintain a dialogue with all students using a journal. Attaching a self-assessment to a summative assessment or having students analyze their growth by comparing their results to a pretest or reviewing a portfolio can produce great realizations for students. A downfall is that students may not receive this vital information until after the summative assessment and are ready to move on to the next topic as a class. The need arises, then, for a self-assessment strategy that can change the culture of assessment in the classroom—a strategy that emphasizes daily self-assessment, that students can understand, that students and teachers can manage time-wise, and most importantly, a strategy that focuses students on the three Sadler questions: Where am I going, where am I now, and how can I close my learning gap?

A Systematic Change

In order for self-assessment to be successful, students must have a clear understanding of the learning targets, understand how to evaluate whether they meet the expectations of the learning target, and be given the opportunity to respond to their conclusions in order to close their personal learning gap.

Where Am I Going?

The first step in changing your classroom to have a greater focus on self-assessment is to place a greater emphasis on learning targets with your students. Research indicates that low achievement is often the outcome of students being unable to understand what teachers expect of them (Black & Wiliam, 1998); students who can identify what they are learning significantly outscore those who cannot (Marzano, 2005). Therefore, the skilled use of learning targets will significantly increase the odds of student success.

When integrating learning targets into your self-assessment practice, it is important they be written in language the students can understand. Writing the targets in "I can" statements helps students understand exactly what is expected of them. Table 8.1 (page 192) shows examples of learning targets written in this manner.

Table 8.1: Learning Targets Written as *I Can* Statements

Sixth-Grade Math Prime Time Unit	Tenth-Grade Chemistry Chemical Reactions Unit
1. I can determine if a number is prime or composite.	1. I can identify synthesis reactions.
2. I can find the prime factorization of any number.	2. I can identify decomposition reactions.
3. I can find the greatest common factor of a set of numbers.	3. I can identify single and double replacement reactions.
4. I can reduce fractions to simplest form.	4. I can identify combustion reactions.
5. Given a fraction, decimal, or percent, I can find the other two.	5. I can predict the products of combustion reactions.
6. I can find the least common multiple of a set of numbers.	6. I can predict the products of single and double replacement reactions.
7. I can find the least common denominator of two fractions.	7. I can write chemical equations in words.
8. I can compare and order fractions.	8. I can write chemical equations in symbols.
	9. I can balance chemical equations.

Once we have written the learning targets in an easily understandable form for students, we must systematize their use, so it becomes part of the classroom's culture. To do this, choose no more than one or two targets to be the primary focus of a class period. Begin each period with those learning targets. List the targets of focus on the front board and, as students settle in, share the expectation that they will write the targets in their planners or assignment notebooks. This helps students answer the first Sadler question, Where am I going? In following this procedure, you will have given a clear statement of what students should be able to do by the end of the class period.

Where Am I Now?

In order for students to address the second Sadler question, the teacher must allow for student reflection during and/or at the end of instruction. By creating a rubric that incorporates all the unit learning targets (fig. 8.1), students can self-assess themselves daily on the learning target(s) of that day.

Name:_____   Date: _____

5—I know how to do this skill, and I can teach it to another person. I need to practice this skill every now and then, so I do not forget how to do it correctly.

4—I know how to do this skill, but I am not confident enough to teach it to another person. I need to continue practicing this skill.

3—I can do this skill some of the time, but I still make mistakes. I need to practice this skill in order to get better.

2—I have difficulty with this skill and need help from the teacher or another adult to learn how to do it correctly.

1—I am unfamiliar with this skill and need instruction.

Learning Target	Trial 1	Trial 2	Trial 3	Trial 4	Trial 5
1. I can determine if a number is prime or composite.					
2. I can find the prime factorization of any number.					
3. I can find the greatest common factor of a set of numbers.					
4. I can reduce fractions to simplest form.					
5. Given a fraction, decimal, or percent, I can find the other two.					
6. I can find the least common multiple of a set of numbers.					
7. I can find the least common denominator of two fractions.					
8. I can compare and order fractions.					

Figure 8.1: A daily self-assessment.

Certain conditions have to be in place for this to be successful with your class, however. First of all, students must understand that this is not a graded activity; they need to understand this activity will truly help them identify what they know and what they don't know. Second, the rating scale students use to assess themselves needs to be clear and worded in such a way that students are not threatened by the language. A "1" in this case is not a failing mark, but rather a way for students to articulate to the teacher and themselves that they are unfamiliar with the skill and need instruction to improve.

Students often do not want to give themselves the lowest score on a rating scale, even if that is where they are. Knowing this, on the first day of using this system, ask the students to rate themselves on the learning target for the day, before any instruction. Give the students a short 5-point quiz on the learning targets. Naturally, most will do poorly. Then ask to see their self-assessments and take note of how students have rated themselves. Go through the definitions with the class and ask, "Did you make a proper assessment of your current knowledge?" Many students will see the disconnect between their self-assessment and the definitions; this opens the door for a dialogue to help the entire class achieve a better understanding. You can then explain why students will use this sheet on a daily basis to help them identify their learning gaps.

How Am I Going to Close the Gap?

Addressing the last Sadler question is often the hardest. When students know what their gaps are, however, it's much easier. When using a system like the one described earlier, students are continually reflecting on their learning and can see their strengths and weaknesses. Therefore, when a teacher offers remediation after school, differentiates learning during class time, or offers other opportunities for students to target the areas in which they need the most growth, the students know where to focus their attention. You move toward *facilitating* rather than leading individualized learning because the student is telling you where his or her learning gaps are.

In addition, a self-assessment should be attached to every summative assessment. Begin by having the students analyze their summative assessment performance according to the learning targets. Figure 8.2 shows how to organize this task. It is important to correlate the problems on the assessment to the learning target and to use the same rating scale as the one used on a daily basis in class. *Students must not see themselves as grading their assessment.* They are identifying their strengths and weaknesses, so they can clearly identify their learning gaps.

Name:_____   Date: _____

5—I know how to do this skill, and I can teach it to another person. I need to practice this skill every now and then, so I do not forget how to do it correctly.

4—I know how to do this skill, but I am not confident enough to teach it to another person. I need to continue practicing this skill.

3—I can do this skill some of the time, but I still make mistakes. I need to practice this skill in order to get better.

2—I have difficulty with this skill and need help from the teacher or another adult to learn how to do it correctly.

1—I am unfamiliar with this skill and need instruction.

Learning Target	Problems That Address the Target	Points Possible for the Target	Points I Received	My Self-Assessment
1. I can determine if a number is prime or composite.	1a, 1b, 1c	3		
2. I can find the prime factorization of any number.	2, 3	2		

continued on next page →

Figure 8.2: A summative self-assessment.

Learning Target	Problems That Address the Target	Points Possible for the Target	Points I Received	My Self-Assessment
3. I can find the greatest common factor of a set of numbers.	4, 5, 6	3		
4. I can reduce fractions to simplest form.	7, 8	2		
5. Given a fraction, decimal, or percent, I can find the other two.	9, 10, 11, 12, 13, 14, 15, 16, 25	9		
6. I can find the least common multiple of a set of numbers.	17, 18	2		
7. I can find the least common denominator of two fractions.	19, 20	2		
8. I can compare and order fractions.	21, 22, 23, 24	4		

After completing this self-assessment, students know where their learning gaps are; next, the teacher must give students the opportunity to close those gaps. A couple of self-assessments that students could use to guide them in the process of improving their work are shown in figure 8.3 and figure 8.4 (page 198).

Name:_____

DIRECTIONS: Spend some time looking over your test, and assess your performance by completing the following items. Please take the time to *seriously* reflect on your work, and do your best to offer neatly organized responses.

1. Identify one or two learning targets that were strengths and one or two that were weaknesses. Describe why you believe each one is a strength or weakness.

Strengths

Learning Target	

Weaknesses

Learning Target	

2. As is the case with most tests, all of the learning targets are not represented equally. There may be a learning target you understand at a greater depth than what was tested. On your paper, demonstrate your greater depth of understanding by showing an example and working through it. Please explain your problem, strategy, and solution carefully, so I am convinced of your understanding.

3. Here is your chance to show me that you understand a learning target better than your test showed. Identify one learning target that you did poorly on, and show me that you understand it. Don't forget to show and explain all the work or thinking necessary to find the correct solution.

Source: Adapted from Brown, 2005, p. 69.

Figure 8.3: A self-assessment for reflection on strengths and weaknesses, example 1.

Name:_____ Date:_____ Class:_____

1. After studying _____, I am confident I can do the following learning target(s) successfully.

2. After studying _____, I can do the following learning target(s), but I still need to work on it.

3. After studying _____, I am still struggling with the following learning target(s).

4. There is one learning target I understand better than the test showed.
   a. Learning Target:

   b. Proof of My Understanding:

5. There is one learning target I am going to work to improve on over the next week.
   a. Learning Target:
   b. My Plan:
      - Friday—

      - Saturday—

      - Sunday—

      - Monday—

      - Tuesday—

      - Wednesday—

      - Thursday—

      - Friday—*Mr. Overlie will give me a quiz on this learning target so I can prove my understanding.*

Figure 8.4: A self-assessment for reflection on strengths and weaknesses, example 2.

Next Steps

Teachers have a long list of initiatives they can work on to improve their classroom instruction, but using formative assessment that emphasizes student self-assessment and reflection deserves to be a high priority. When implemented in an organized manner, formative assessment increases student achievement in the classroom and has positive effects on standardized test results. One teacher implementing these strategies is a start, but it is not enough. Students will simply be frustrated if expectations are different in every class they attend. I advocate for a total shift in a school's way of doing business with formative assessment becoming a primary focus of the school's improvement plan and professional development.

Although there are many ways to incorporate self-assessment into the classroom, the most effective strategy is to implement a systematic change. Self-assessment does not need to become an additional step. Instead, it can and should become an integral part of each class that students use to guide themselves through the process of answering, Where am I going, where am I now, and how can I close my learning gap?

References

Andrade, H. (2008). Self-assessment through rubrics. *Educational Leadership, 65*(4), 60–63.

Andrade, H., & Du, Y. (2007). Student responses to criteria-referenced self-assessment. *Assessment and Evaluation in Higher Education, 32*(2), 159–181.

Andrade, H., Du, Y., & Wang, X. (2007, April). *Putting rubrics to the test: A study of the effects of rubric-referenced self-assessment on students' writing.* Paper presented at the annual meeting of the American Educational Research Association, Chicago, Illinois.

Black, P. (1998). Formative assessment: Raising standards inside the classroom. *School Science Review, 80*(291), 39–46.

Black, P., & Wiliam, D. (1998, October). Inside the black box: Raising standards through classroom assessment. *Phi Delta Kappan, 80*(2), 139–147.

Brown, S. (2005). You made it through the test; what about the aftermath? *Mathematics Teaching in the Middle School, 11*(2), 68–73.

Crooks, T. J. (1988). The impact of classroom evaluation practices on students. *Review of Educational Research, 58*(4), 438–481.

D'Arcangelo, M. (1998). The brains behind the brain. *Educational Leadership, 56*(3), 20–25.

Diamond, M., & Hopson, J. (1998). *Magic trees of the mind: How to nurture your child's intelligence, creativity, and healthy emotions from birth through adolescence.* New York: Penguin Putnam.

Leahy, S., Lyon, C., Thompson, M., & Wiliam, D. (2005). Classroom assessment: Minute by minute, day by day. *Educational Leadership, 63*(3), 18–24.

Lewbel, S. R., & Hibbard, K. M. (2001). Are standards and true learning compatible? *Principal Leadership (High School Ed.), 1*(5), 16–20.

MacDonald, B., & Boud, D. (2003). The impact of self-assessment on achievement: The effects of self-assessment training on performance in external examinations. *Assessment in Education, 10*(2), 209–220.

Marzano, R. (2005). *What works in schools: Translating research into action* [PowerPoint presentation]. Accessed at www.marzanoandassociates. com/pdf/latest02.pdf on October 29, 2008.

McTighe, J., & O'Connor, K. (2005, November). Seven practices for effective learning. *Educational Leadership, 63*(3), 10–17.

Natriello, G. (1987). The impact of evaluation process on students. *Educational Psychologist, 22*(2), 155–175.

Ritchhart, R., & Perkins, D. (2008). Making thinking visible. *Educational Leadership, 65*(5), 57–61.

Ross, J. A., Hogaboam-Gray, A., & Rolheiser, C. (2002). Student self-evaluation in grade 5–6 mathematics: Effects on problem-solving achievement. *Educational Assessment, 8*(1), 43–59.

Sadler, D. R. (1989). Formative assessment and the design of instructional systems. *Instructional Science, 18,* 145–165.

Stiggins, R. (2005, December). From formative assessment to assessment for learning: A path to success in standards-based schools. *Phi Delta Kappan, 87*(4), 324–328.

Stiggins, R., Arter, J., Chappuis, J., & Chappuis, S. (2004). *Classroom assessment* for *student learning: Doing it right—Using it well.* Portland, OR: ETS Assessment Training Institute.

Wiliam, D., Lee, C., Harrison, C., & Black, P. (2004, March). Teachers developing assessment for learning: Impact on student achievement. *Assessment in Education, 11*(1), 49–65.

White, B. Y., & Frederiksen, J. R. (1998). Inquiry, modeling, and metacognition: Making science accessible to all students. *Cognition and Instruction, 16*(1), 3–118.

Wiggins, G., & McTighe, J. (2005). *Understanding by design.* Alexandria, VA: Association for Supervision and Curriculum Development.

Wolfe, P., & Brandt, R. (1998). What do we know from brain research? *Educational Leadership, 56*(3), 8–13.

NICOLE M. VAGLE

Nicole Vagle is an independent consultant and president of Lighthouse Learning Community, Inc. Nicole was formerly a high school reform specialist for Minneapolis Public Schools, where she worked closely with school and district staff to support the implementation of small learning communities. This high school reform work also included coaching individuals and teams of secondary administrators and teachers in examining data and promoting high expectations for all students. Nicole was also the training coordinator for the Osseo (Minnesota) Area Schools' Data Program Templates Project in collaboration with the University of Minnesota. As training coordinator, she helped elementary and secondary educators design templates to track and analyze data. Intrigued by the powerful impact teacher leaders have in schools and districts, she later became a program evaluator and trainer at the Princeton Center for Leadership Training in New Jersey. Nicole produced a training DVD that illustrates a protocol for examining the effectiveness of assessments and student learning. She continues to work with schools and districts nationwide to increase understanding of developing and using assessments to promote student learning. She is a contributor to *The Principal as Assessment Leader* (Solution Tree, 2009).

NINE

Inspiring and Requiring Action

Nicole M. Vagle

Since the advent of formal education in the United States, both the educational system and that system's every reform have been premised on adults' notions of how education should be conceptualized and practiced. Educators unequivocally agree that students and their learning are why we exist, yet we rarely embrace students as partners on their learning journey. There is something fundamentally amiss about building and rebuilding an entire system without consulting at any point those it is ostensibly designed to serve.

—Alison Cook-Sather

The best ally we have in motivating students to learn and helping them succeed may be the students themselves. When teachers partner with students, new insights emerge that build a positive classroom culture filled with hope and possibility.

A visit I made to a high school science classroom reflected the potential of this partnership. The teacher began the class by going over the various parts of a lab report. Then students were asked to write a report on the lab they had conducted the day before. Observing a young man with his head down near the back of the room, I decided to make myself useful. I spent the next thirty minutes trying to pull ideas and writing out of this young man. He was thoroughly disgruntled with me, alternating his responses between "I don't care" and "This is stupid!"

He was completely lost when we tackled the analysis section in which he was to explain the difference between a chemical and physical reaction. Then I pulled a few of his peers around our table and had a conversation. His teacher later reported that this was the only assignment this young man handed in the whole year. Upon further review, it was evident that his "I don't cares" were really "I don't knows."

Of course, teachers don't have thirty minutes to spend with each student every day to figure out what will open the door for learning. However, when teachers intentionally partner with students and structure conversations and activities around learning targets that are essential for achieving the standard and being successful on the assessment, they create systems that will help all students achieve at high levels.

What could these conversations and activities look like if teachers intentionally "invited"—that is, *required*—students to become partners in their learning and achievement? When teachers share responsibility for learning with students, achievement, motivation, and engagement increase (Black & Wiliam, 1998; Carini, Kuh, & Klein, 2004; Hattie & Timperley, 2007; Saphier, 2005; Stiggins, Arter, Chappuis, & Chappuis, 2005; Wiliam, 2007). In this chapter, I will briefly review some of the most compelling research underlying student involvement in assessment practice and share practical strategies for using descriptive feedback and error analysis to bring students in as partners on their learning journey.

The Case for Involving Students in Assessment

Historically, the process of assessing and offering feedback has exclusively been the role of the teacher. Teachers spend countless hours thinking about, commenting on, and planning for student learning. By the time they hand back an assessment, they have deep insight about what students need to do next. Frustration mounts when students don't act on these insights, however, and their inaction is often chalked up to laziness or lack of desire. But what if students' lack of action stems from not understanding what to do or how to do it? We often give them little or no time to do their own thinking about, commenting on, or planning for their learning. Imagine a new model of assessing and offering feedback in which students work as hard as if not harder than teachers, and classroom instruction includes activities that ask students to learn how to assess and give feedback on their own and others' work.

Royce Sadler (1989) framed three questions to help students conceptualize the assessment process: Where am I going? Where am I now? How can I close the gap? Other researchers have used these questions as a starting point for their own explorations of the notion of student involvement in assessment.

Rick Stiggins, Judith Arter, Jan Chappuis, and Steve Chappuis (2005) position student involvement as one of five keys to quality assessment. Student involvement means, first, that students understand the learning target (where they are going). Then they use the data from assessments—both formal (tests, quizzes, papers) and informal (discussion, observations of student words and actions)—to identify and reflect on their strengths and weaknesses (where they are now) and to set goals for the next steps toward proficiency (closing the gap).

The research overwhelmingly identifies quality feedback as a major factor in increasing student learning (Black, Harrison, Lee, Marshall, & Wiliam, 2003; Guskey, 2002; Hattie & Timperley, 2007; Marzano, 2007; Reeves, 2007; Wiliam, 2007). Moreover, poor feedback practices can have an adverse impact on student learning. Feedback used incorrectly "is worse than a waste of the teacher's time and energy: Ineffective feedback is inversely related to student achievement" (Reeves, 2007, pp. 229–230). John Hattie and Helen Timperley (2007) conducted a meta-analysis of effective feedback practices and found that using descriptive feedback practices affected student achievement twice as much as the average educational intervention. Like Stiggins and his associates, Hattie and Timperley used Sadler's questions to frame quality feedback practices. They came to the "critical conclusion" that

> teachers need to seek and learn from feedback (such as students' responses to tests) as much as do students, and only when assessment provides such learning is it of value to either. . . . In too many cases, testing is used as the measure to judge whether change has occurred rather than as a mechanism to further enhance and consolidate learning by teachers or students. (p. 104)

The notion of partnership is inherent in this statement; that is, both teachers and students collect, exchange, and act on feedback. In this partnership, learning takes place not only "in" the student, but also in the relationship between the teacher and the student. Teachers and students bring unique perspectives to the examination of assessment results. This exchange is the foundation of student involvement.

Involving students in their learning is a key characteristic of formative assessment that has yielded positive results (Black & Wiliam, 1998; Wiliam, 2007). *Formative assessment* has been defined and interpreted in many ways. The general notion is that teachers use assessment data from quizzes, tests, student writing, observations, and other methods of assessment to plan instructional activities that help students address their misunderstandings or extend their learning. Most importantly, students become involved by using these assessment data to articulate their strengths and identify their next steps in progressing toward the intended learning. Marnie Thompson and Dylan Wiliam (2007) also use Sadler's three questions as a framework for formative assessment practice. In fact, they explicitly advocate for teachers to activate students as owners of their own learning. The focus on the learner as a separate and equally important user of formative assessment data underscores the power of students as partners in their learning.

Student Involvement in the Classroom

Two important ways to involve students in assessment are the practices of *descriptive feedback* and *error analysis*. These practices require both teachers and students to reflect on Sadler's three questions, Where am I going? Where am I now? How can I close the gap? In order for this reflection to produce increased student achievement, teachers and students must identify the "how" in the third question and act on it.

Descriptive Feedback

As an English teacher, I spent countless hours offering my students detailed commentary on their papers. In fact, I was working considerably harder than my students in analyzing their work! Although I assumed they would act on my feedback, I could have intentionally *structured* opportunities for them to analyze and think deeply about their work and then followed up with affirmation or redirection as needed. Not only would I have lightened my load, but also I would have created a valuable problem-solving endeavor to build my students' capacity to become independently critical writers.

In order to shift some of the important thinking about learning to students, feedback must be more than just a transmittal from teacher to student. It must become a process that connects teachers to students, students to students, and students to themselves. Carol Rodgers (2006) describes it well:

> It is not an evaluation of good and bad but an exploration of what helps and hinders learning and why. In all, feedback gives everyone the chance to slow down, to breathe, to make sense of where they've been, how they got there, where they should go next, and the best ways

to get there together—a decision made with students, rather than for students. (p. 219)

As I learned firsthand, when we offer feedback for the purpose of increasing learning, we must *inspire* and *require* action. Students must very clearly understand what the intended learning looks like, and they must identify the very next step in their learning. If students understand what to do, they can be *inspired* to take that next step. If these next steps are *required*—and teachers provide the time, structure, and support for students to act on the feedback— increased learning will follow (Hattie & Timperley, 2007).

Characteristics of Descriptive Feedback

The qualities of descriptive feedback became even clearer to me after an interaction with my daughter, Maya, when she was in second grade. On Wednesday of each week, students in her classroom received an object and were asked to create something and write about it using details. They brought the "imagination creation" and description back to school on Friday to share it with their peers. Maya brought her writing home on Monday, and usually the feedback the teacher provided was "Super Job." After Maya had been doing these imagination creations for about two months, I looked at her writing more closely and was struck by a few things. While she included some specific details, she also had spaces and capital letters in the middle of words that made it more difficult to understand. As a former English teacher and her mother, I decided to ask her about it. Her response was laced with exasperation as she exclaimed, "Mom, it doesn't matter! Miss Johnson puts 'Super Job' on it anyway."

The qualities of descriptive feedback that promotes learning and not just compliance or efforts toward a better grade are as follows.

Descriptive feedback describes learning; it doesn't quantify or evaluate it. Grades, percentages, smiley faces, and nonspecific criticism ("try harder," "try again," "missing") do not describe learning but quantify it. Ruth Butler (1988) studied the impact of giving grades on learning. Students were given a book with a range of activities on a certain topic. The work was collected and graded. Then, students were randomly divided into three groups that were each given a different type of feedback: marks/grades only, feedback comments only, or marks/grades and comments. A few weeks later, students were given a similar set of tasks and told they would receive the same type of feedback. Students receiving marks/grades only and both marks/grades and comments made no progress in achievement, but students receiving only comments gained an average of 30 percent. Anne Davies (2007) suggests that the common practice of giving students comments and grades/marks simultaneously could be slightly modified so that students would receive only comments to begin with, and the grade/mark would be delayed a few days, giving students time to act on the feedback in order to improve their work.

Descriptive feedback describes strengths in terms of the learning criteria (Hattie & Timperley, 2007; Marzano, 2007; Reeves, 2007). In reflecting on my feedback practices as a teacher, I recall writing "excellent" or "creative" on papers many times. While offered with the best intention, the message was general and not focused on the learning criteria that would help students identify their strengths. I knew what was excellent and why, but did my students?

Descriptive feedback provides next steps for specific action (Davies, 2007; Wiliam, 2007). Comments such as "check your work," "explain," or "many fragments" identify the beginning of the next step, but more detailed and active statements give students clear ideas about how to confidently make progress toward the intended learning:

- "In the analysis section of your lab report, explain how the results in your data table support your hypothesis."

- "Find and fix three sentence fragments."

- "Use two words from our math word wall to describe how you came to the answer to problem #3."

Descriptive feedback is focused and manageable. Teachers should identify one to two next steps so that students see possibility and have hope of being able to learn and actually accomplish the next step in their learning (Stiggins et al., 2005).

Descriptive feedback is timely (Reeves, 2007). When feedback is provided after the learning is supposed to have taken place (that is, after the grade is final), the motivation to learn from it is drastically reduced, as students see the grade/mark as an ending, not as part of a cyclical process designed to improve learning (Hattie & Timperley, 2007). In addition, if too much time passes between the assessment and the feedback, students may be in a different spot on the learning journey, making the feedback inaccurate and confusing.

In general, effective descriptive feedback does the following:

- Helps students understand and articulate more deeply the intended learning (Where am I going?)

- Helps students determine where they are and their very next step (Where am I now?)

- Helps students understand the steps toward achieving the intended learning (How can I close the gap?)

While feedback from teacher to student is a common occurrence, in true student-involved assessment, students learn the characteristics of quality descriptive feedback and practice providing that kind of feedback to their peers. Furthermore, students learn how to self-assess—to identify the strengths in their own work and the areas in which they need to improve—and to determine for themselves the next steps they should take.

Classroom Examples of Descriptive Feedback

Knowing the qualities of effective descriptive feedback, we might revisit the episode when Maya dismissed my attempts to encourage quality writing. If the teacher had realized that the students had lost sight of the reason they were writing these "imagination creation" descriptions, what might her feedback have looked like? How could she have brought the students into the descriptive feedback process so that she wasn't the only one who knew and could articulate their strengths and next steps? Figure 9.1 describes a possible descriptive feedback activity in which students and teachers are both actively involved in the process.

Step 1. Helping Students Understand the Intended Learning

In small groups, Maya's teacher asks students to brainstorm the following: *What is quality writing? What does quality writing look like?*

As a whole class, Maya and her peers come to consensus on two or three of the most essential criteria and brainstorm "quality" and "not yet" (that is, not quite quality) descriptions of writing.

Step 2. Helping Students Understand the Intended Learning and the Steps in the Journey

Using a sample piece of writing, small groups of students identify the following:

- Two strengths of the sample and evidence to support
- One area to work on and evidence to support
- One possible next step in the area to work on

The strengths and areas to work on come from the criteria and descriptions of quality writing in Step 1. The evidence to support comes directly from the writing in the sample.

continued on next page →

Figure 9.1: Descriptive feedback on the imagination creation assessment.

Step 3. Helping Students Determine Where They Are on the Journey and Their Next Steps

Students then review their own writing. First, they identify two strengths in their writing and evidence to support. Then, they identify one area to focus on, the evidence that led them to that area, and their very next step.

Step 4. Inspiring and Requiring Action

After Maya and her peers have identified necessary revisions in their own writing, the teacher posts the quality writing criteria in different areas of the room. Students move to the area of the room where the criterion they need to work on is posted. The teacher has prepared a brief activity for each criterion. For example, students who need to work on organization may receive a list of sentences to revise into a paragraph that has a beginning, middle, and end. Once they have created the paragraph together, they check their work against a model paragraph the teacher provides. Then, the small group discusses and records the similarities and differences between their paragraph and the model paragraph. Once the students have worked through the group activity, they return to their desks to make revisions in their own writing.

Note: While this example represents an elementary activity, these steps may be applied to any grade level or content area. The creative writing sample would be replaced with, for example, the analysis section of a lab report or a constructed-response question from an exam.

The next classroom example illustrates how to help students understand the intended learning criteria more clearly, how students can provide one another with descriptive feedback, and how students can self-assess by identifying strengths and next steps based on a new and deeper understanding of the criteria. In this classroom, students took a seven-question quiz after reading a newspaper article. The students struggled to effectively respond to the following constructed-response item, which was intended to measure their comprehension of text:

> The author of this article states that it is "pointless to lay blame" for the sports facilities mess. However, he does

indicate some possible causes. In your own words, state at least three causes of the stadium mess that the author mentions. (Minnesota Department of Education, 2000)

The next day was designed to help students learn what a quality response looks like for this text-based assessment (see fig. 9.2, page 214).

Using the process in figures 9.1 and 9.2 affords students the opportunity to give, receive, and act on feedback on a constructed-response quiz, the written analysis section of a lab report, the introduction to a persuasive essay, a political cartoon, or other student work. When students engage in this type of dialogue, they are set up to be able to confidently answer Sadler's three questions that promote student involvement.

The next classroom example comes from Vicki Barry, a mathematics teacher at Goodrich Middle School in Nebraska. She implemented a descriptive feedback process for homework with her sixth-graders. She described the process in an action research report:

A normal day in my classroom would begin with a warm up, which consisted of an activity or problem to get my students engaged and interested in the daily objective. Then after about five minutes, we would have a class discussion over some examples on how to solve the problems for that objective. At the end of the hour, which was approximately the last 15–20 minutes of the class, we focused on homework. Students would go over and check the previous day's homework by showing how they completed certain problems to the class and then I would end the hour by summarizing the daily objective and assigning the next homework. The students would have approximately the last five to ten minutes in class to work on this assignment which would be due the following day.

Step 1. Helping Students Understand the Intended Learning

Students are asked to individually write their interpretations of the learning target being measured in the constructed-response question. In this case, the students receive the following statement to interpret: "I can comprehend nonfiction text, which means I can summarize the arguments outlined in the text." Then, students meet in small groups of three to four to share their individual interpretations and come to consensus on one definition. Each small group posts its definition, and the class discusses the similarities and differences among the definitions. The most essential characteristics generated from the discussion are posted in the room.

Step 2. Helping Students Understand the Intended Learning and the Steps in the Journey

Back in small groups, students receive five sample student responses of varying quality. They determine the strengths and weaknesses of each sample and rank them in order from 1 (strongest) to 5 (weakest). The small groups share their rankings and the accompanying explanations, while the teacher highlights the descriptions that represent quality and prompts the class to identify specific parts of the samples that support their claims. Then, individually or in small groups, students choose one of the weaker examples, identify its strengths, come up with suggestions on how to make it better, and revise the sample to make it stronger.

Step 3. Helping Students Determine Where They Are on the Journey and Their Next Steps

Students revisit their own responses written during the quiz. Based on their new understanding of the intended learning, students self-assess by identifying their strengths and next steps.

Step 4. Inspiring and Requiring Action

Students are required to make the necessary revisions either during class or by a specified due date. Teachers administer another constructed response on a different text to check the effectiveness of the activity and ensure that students can now independently comprehend text.

Figure 9.2: Descriptive feedback on a text-based assessment.

When I began my action research study, the end of the hour for homework time dramatically changed. Since my study involved having students give their peers feedback on their homework assignments, I had to plan my hour accordingly so there would be enough time after instruction to follow through with the feedback process. I felt I needed 25–30 minutes initially, so it took three days for me to adjust my instruction time properly to allot enough time for students to be introduced to the process. When I finally altered my lesson correctly, I passed out the feedback forms [see figure 9.3, page 217] to my students after the daily objective lesson and gave them instructions on how the process was going to work.

Once the students exchanged their papers and had their names on the feedback forms, I would go over the assignment's answers. . . . The students had to give feedback on three problems which I chose because I felt those problems were the most significant to the objective. If students did not know how to solve the problem, or what to say for feedback, we would discuss the problem as a class on the board.

After the students gave feedback to their peers on the forms and nobody had more questions, I would have the students pass back the papers with the forms to their peers. Then, I would give everyone two to three minutes to look over their comments and to write a quick reflection on how the feedback helped them learn or fix their mistakes [figure 9.3]. At the end of the hour, the students would then pass their papers in to me so I could review them. Then, the students began working on the next assignment for the following day after we summarized the objective.

By the end of the study, this process changed for the better. After a couple of weeks of modeling and practice, it did not take as much time as it did in the beginning. In the beginning I had to allot 25–30 minutes of class time, whereas in the end, I only allotted 10 minutes. I also stopped telling the class which three problems the students had to give their peer feedback on because the students and I found it much more effective if they were able to choose the three problems that their peer missed. (Barry, 2008, pp. 18–20; used with permission)

The homework completion rate in this class increased from 50 percent to 77 percent (twenty-two students) within the first four feedback sessions. In addition, Barry observed that "the students . . . went from stressing about giving feedback to begging for it when they did not receive any" (2008, p. 33). In terms of achievement, 80 percent or more of students were proficient on all eighteen objectives. In this scenario, descriptive feedback became a consistent process in which both students and teacher shared the responsibility for learning from the homework.

When students are active partners in this descriptive feedback process, they have ownership of their learning and increased motivation and engagement (Davies, 2007). Descriptive feedback is motivational because it provides hope for the students and concrete direction in how to make their work better. If this is to be an authentic partnership, then both teachers *and* students share the roles of analyzing work, identifying strengths, identifying next steps, and revising the work appropriately. In order to bring students in as partners in their learning, we must provide opportunities for them to become actively involved and reflective in the feedback process.

Error Analysis

Descriptive feedback involves identifying what students understand and what they need to do next to further their learning. Student errors can offer much insight into the breakdown in learning and what students need to do to fix it. Mistakes, in essence, are rich areas for learning. Thomas Guskey (2007, pp. 23–24) states:

Descriptive Feedback

Name:_____   Date: _____

Objective:_____

Problem # _____ Feedback

_____

_____

_____

Problem # _____ Feedback

_____

_____

_____

Problem # _____ Feedback

_____

_____

_____

. . . .

Reflection: What do you think about the feedback you received? Has it helped you? Explain why or why not.

_____

_____

_____

Source: Barry, 2008, appendix B, p. 38. Used with permission.

Figure 9.3: Student feedback form.

What better learning–to–learn skill is there than learning from one's mistakes? Mistakes should not mark the end of learning; rather, they can be the beginning. Some assessment experts argue, in fact, that students learn nothing from a successful performance. Instead, they learn when their performance is less than successful, for then they can gain direction about how to improve (Wiggins, 1998).

To learn from mistakes, students must go beyond simple identification of right and wrong or strong and weak. John Hattie and Helen Timperley (2007) describe the importance of guiding students to understand not only what they got wrong but also why they got it wrong and how to fix it. Teachers can facilitate this learning by asking students to examine mistakes with questions like, What happened? Why? How can I do it differently next time? Structuring this type of thinking fosters partnership with students in that teachers are asking (and requiring) them to think about their learning.

Depending on the type of assessment, analyzing errors may take on many different forms. Consider the following scenarios.

Scenario 1

Second-graders are asked to do five math problems for homework. As students walk in the next day, the teacher glances over their homework and chooses the item that students have struggled with most frequently. She displays figure 9.4 for the whole class and asks individual students to spend some time analyzing the mistake and providing some insight into next steps. Then, in small groups or as a whole class, students share their thinking and problem-solving strategies. This example illustrates one way students and teachers analyze errors by figuring out what went wrong and why, explaining how to fix it, and strategizing what to do differently next time.

Scenario 2

Brooke Davis and Trevor Smith, teachers at Davison High School in Michigan, structure error analysis opportunities for students based on their incorrect responses on a multiple-choice quiz. Figure 9.5 shows three of the twelve questions on a geologic timeline quiz.

$8.92
-$6.25
$14.67

Is this answer correct?

Why or why not?

What advice would you offer this student to help her avoid making the same mistake again?

Figure 9.4: Second-grade math activity from homework.

Identify the choice that best completes the statement or answers the question.

1. While looking for fossils on an eroded hillside, you discover fossil coral and fish in one layer. In a layer just above, you find the fossil imprint of a fern frond and some fossilized moss. Assuming the rock has not been disturbed, which of the following is the most probable conclusion?
   a. The area had been a sea until recent times.
   b. A forest had once grown there but had become submerged by water.
   c. In ancient times a sea had been replaced by land.
   d. A saltwater sea had changed to a freshwater lake long ago.

2. According to Figure 14.1, what was the earliest form of multicellular life on earth?
   a. Fish
   b. Invertebrates—jellyfish
   c. Land plants
   d. Reptiles

3. According to Figure 14.1, what is the correct chronological development of organisms?
   a. Birds, dinosaurs, jawed fish, prokaryotes
   b. Dinosaurs, jawed fish, birds, prokaryotes
   c. Jawed fish, dinosaurs, prokaryotes, birds
   d. Prokaryotes, jawed fish, dinosaurs, birds

Source: Davis, B., & Smith, T. Davison High School, Davison, Michigan, 2007. Used with permission.

Figure 9.5: A quiz on the geologic timeline and the origin of life.

After students have taken the quiz, they receive it back with items marked correct or incorrect. In addition, they receive the key shown in figure 9.6, which offers more information on each item: the learning objective, the correct answer, and a description of where to study or a clue as to where the misunderstanding occurred based on the incorrect answer students chose.

1. Answer: c. The Law of Superposition holds that more recent layers are closer to the surface. *(Bloom's Level B; Standard B5)*

Answer	Feedback
a.	Think about what fern and moss layers above the marine layer indicate.
b.	Remember that the older layers are on the bottom and the new form on top.
c.	Correct!
d.	Consider the presence of terrestrial fossils.

2. Answer: b. Invertebrates, here represented by jellyfishes, are graphed closest to the original one-celled life forms. *(Bloom's Level C; Standard B5)*

Answer	Feedback
a.	Look carefully at the dates on the horizontal axis of the graph.
b.	Correct!
c.	Land plants didn't appear until the Paleozoic era.
d.	Reptiles are relatively complex and didn't appear until about 245 million years ago.

3. Answer: d. This option presents organisms in the order they appear in the graph. *(Bloom's Level A; Standard B5)*

Answer	Feedback
a.	Remember simplest forms of life existed first.
b.	The earliest life forms were single-celled.
c.	Complex animals like fish and dinosaurs evolved later than simple prokaryotes.
d.	That's right.

Figure 9.6: Answer key and error analysis.

The purpose of this quiz is for teachers and students to understand what learning has been achieved and what needs more work. With the quiz and error analysis in hand, students could capitalize on their mistakes by doing one or more of the following:

- **Create questions.** Students create questions that would make their incorrect response correct.

- **Write an explanation.** Students identify two questions they got wrong or struggled with the most. Using the tip provided in the feedback column, students describe their mistake and what they have learned about this question.

- **Develop student tips.** Teachers leave the feedback column blank and have students work in groups to complete the tips that would help students understand their mistake.

Finally, using evidence from the quiz and the follow-up activity, students identify their strengths and areas that need focus. Then students are asked to make a plan that determines what they do next to understand the intended learning.

When teachers structure opportunities for students to analyze their mistakes, students are much more involved in thinking about and planning for their learning. As students discuss their errors with one another, it is an opportunity for teachers to eavesdrop on this dialogue. These conversations among students may provide teachers new thoughts and perspectives about how to support student learning.

Scenario 3

After fourth-graders take a formative multiple-choice math test, teachers identify the item that most students got wrong. Then, in small groups the very next day, students analyze the item following the directions in figure 9.7 (page 222). In this example of error analysis, students discuss possible reasons for choosing each of the answers (A, B, C, or D). All students benefit

Purpose: To understand and demonstrate problem solving with whole numbers, fractions, decimals, and integers, specifically determining an amount (cost, recipe, yardage)

Read the problem, select an answer, and then explain how you got your answer.

1. In a group of 8 people, 5 are wearing hats. What fractional part of the group is wearing hats?

    a. 2/8

    b. 3/5

    c. 5/8

    d. 8/5

    Explain.

    _____

    _____

2. In groups of three or four, discuss how you might get each possible answer:

    a.

    b.

    c.

    d.

3. Which is the right answer? _____

4. What two (2) tips would you offer your classmates in order to help them solve this problem correctly?

    _____

    _____

Figure 9.7: Fractions and problem-solving response.

in this error analysis activity; those students who originally got this question wrong analyze the item and discuss explanations for their mistakes with peers in student-friendly language that they may be able to better understand. Students who answered correctly analyze the item in new ways and try to explain incorrect responses.

Teachers may group students by the answer they selected. Then, each group of students participates in an activity that addresses the misunderstanding revealed by the answer chosen. The group of students who selected the correct answer engages in an extension activity.

When teachers use items or responses from the assessment itself as the basis of learning activities that help students understand their mistakes, these errors inspire rich discussion among students. When students become actively engaged in these discussions, they take on some of the ownership in addressing their mistakes and furthering their learning.

Closing Thoughts

This chapter looks at the research describing student involvement in assessment and its effectiveness, discusses the ways that descriptive feedback and error analysis relate to student involvement, and provides concrete examples of how such student involvement looks in the classroom.

When teachers think about involving students, they inevitably see time as a barrier. While the ideas presented here initially do take more time to implement, when students learn how to think about their thinking and learning, we can "cover" much more, and students will learn more deeply. It is my hope that the ideas reflected in this chapter inspire teachers to pause and imagine how students can become active partners in their learning for the purpose of increased student achievement, motivation, and confidence.

References

Barry, V. J. (2008). *Using feedback in a sixth grade mathematics classroom.* Unpublished manuscript from the department of mathematics, University of Nebraska-Lincoln. Accessed at http://scimath.unl.edu/MIM/files/research/BarryV.pdf on February 27, 2009.

Black, P., Harrison, C., Lee, C., Marshall, B., & Wiliam, D. (2003). *Assessment for learning: Putting it into practice.* London: Open University.

Black, P. J., & Wiliam, D. (1998). Inside the black box: Raising standards through classroom assessment. *Phi Delta Kappan, 80*(2), 139–148.

Butler, R. (1988). Enhancing and undermining intrinsic motivation: The effects of task-involving and ego-involving evaluation on interest and performance. *British Journal of Educational Psychology, 78*(3), 210–216.

Carini, R. M., Kuh, G. D., & Klein, S. P. (2004). Student engagement and student learning: Testing the linkages. *Journal of Higher Education,* in press. (First presented at the American Educational Research Association Conference, San Diego, CA, April, 2004.)

Davies, A. (2007). Involving students in the classroom assessment process. In D. Reeves (Ed.), *Ahead of the curve: The power of assessment to transform teaching and learning* (pp. 31–58). Bloomington, IN: Solution Tree.

Guskey, T. R. (2002). *How's my kid doing? A parents' guide to grades, marks, and report cards.* San Francisco: Jossey-Bass.

Guskey, T. (2007). Using assessments to improve teaching and learning. In D. Reeves (Ed.), *Ahead of the curve: The power of assessment to transform teaching and learning* (pp. 15–29). Bloomington, IN: Solution Tree.

Hattie, J., & Timperley, H. (2007). The power of feedback. *Review of Educational Research, 77*(1), 81–112.

Marzano, R. J. (2007). *The art and science of teaching.* Alexandria, VA: Association for Supervision and Curriculum Development.

Minnesota Department of Education. (2000). *Grade 10 Reading MCA II item sampler.* Roseville, MN: Author.

Reeves, D. (Ed.). (2007). *Ahead of the curve: The power of assessment to transform teaching and learning.* Bloomington, IN: Solution Tree.

Rodgers, C. (2006). Attending to student voice: The impact of descriptive feedback on learning and teaching. *Curriculum Inquiry, 36*(2), 209–237.

Sadler, D. R. (1989, March). Formative assessment: Revisiting the territory. *Assessment in Education, 5(1),* 77–84.

Saphier, J. (2005). Masters of motivation. In R. DuFour, R. Eaker, & R. DuFour (Eds.), *On common ground: The power of professional learning communities* (pp. 85–114). Bloomington, IN: Solution Tree (formerly National Educational Service).

Stiggins, R. J., Arter, J., Chappuis, J., & Chappuis, S. (2005). *Classroom assessment* for *student learning: Doing it right—Using it well.* Portland, OR: ETS Assessment Training Institute.

Thompson, M., & Wiliam, D. (2007). *Tight but loose: A conceptual framework for scaling up school reforms.* Paper presented at the annual conference of the American Educational Research Association, Chicago, IL.

Wiliam, D. (2007). Keeping learning on track: Classroom assessment and the regulation of learning. In F. K. Lester Jr. (Ed.), *Second handbook of mathematics teaching and learning* (pp. 1053–1098). Greenwich, CT: Information Age Publishing.

SHARON V. KRAMER

 Dr. Sharon V. Kramer served as assistant superintendent for curriculum and instruction of Kildeer Countryside School District 96 in Buffalo Grove, Illinois. She has completed assessment trainings by Rick Stiggins, Steve Chappuis, Larry Ainsworth, and the Center for Performance Assessment. Dr. Kramer also worked with schools and districts across North America to determine their power standards and develop assessments. Dr. Kramer has presented sessions at state and national conferences sponsored by the National Staff Development Council, National Association for Gifted Children, American Federation of Teachers, and California State University. She is a contributor to *The Collaborative Teacher: Working Together as a Professional Learning Community* (2008).

Linda DuBose

A veteran educator who has taught students in grades kindergarten through eight, Linda DuBose has spent thirty-one years teaching students in urban and suburban school districts. Her experiences have included classroom teacher, gifted program teacher, literacy support teacher, and technology facilitator. She has an extensive background in gifted education, differentiation, literacy, and technology implementation in the classroom. She has presented at national and state conferences and conducted district workshops.

TEN

Engaging the Nintendo Generation

Sharon V. Kramer With Linda DuBose

I have come to realize that truly productive assessment cannot merely be about the qualities of the instruments and the attributes of their resulting scores. Rather, it must also be about the impact of that score ON THE LEARNER.

—Rick Stiggins

Students in today's classrooms are poised to take ownership of their learning. As members of the Nintendo generation, they understand the concept of beating your own score to reach the next level, and as players, they are highly motivated and engaged. In games, they clearly understand the goal or target and problem solve to reach the next level. They will ask others about the codes needed and will remember and apply these complex codes as they play. Even those labeled *reluctant readers* or *unmotivated students* will pore over pages of game code in order to reach the next level. If only we could inspire students to generate the same enthusiasm and perseverance in response to their learning results in the classroom!

Fortunately, we can. Students ask themselves three questions as they remain engaged in their video game quest to reach the highest level: Where am I going? Where am I now? How can I get to the top? Royce Sadler (1989) identified these same three questions as a way to define the information students need to make learning progress in the classroom. When students understand that the purpose of assessment is to answer these questions, they will become more involved in the assessment process. Table 10.1 shows the specific forms such involvement can take (Sadler, 1989; Stiggins, Arter, Chappuis, & Chappuis, 2004). This chapter will outline the research on each of these aspects of student-involved assessment and will provide practical classroom strategies that can be implemented immediately to bring students into the assessment process.

Table 10.1: Guiding Questions for Student Involvement

Student Question	Student Involvement
Where am I going?	Students articulate a clear and understandable vision of the learning target.
	Students understand examples and models of strong and weak work.
Where am I now?	Students receive regular descriptive feedback.
	Students self-assess and set goals.
How can I close the gap?	Students support one another in addressing gaps in their learning.
	Students track progress and communicate their learning.

The Role of Assessment

There are three categories of classroom assessments: diagnostic, formative, and summative (O'Connor, 2007b). *Diagnostic* assessments (pre-assessments) precede instruction to provide information in planning and guiding differentiated instruction. *Formative* assessments (*for* learning) occur concurrently with instruction, are ongoing, and provide descriptive feedback along the way. *Summative* assessments (*of* learning) occur at the conclusion of an instructional segment.

Diagnostic assessments provide students with a starting point and act as a guide to measure progress. Formative assessment allows students to monitor progress along the way as a check of their understanding. Formative assessments are defined as "all those activities undertaken by teachers and students that provide information to be used as feedback to enhance learning and achievement. Assessment *for* learning is students and teachers using evidence of learning to adapt teaching and learning to meet immediate learning needs minute-by-minute and day-by-day" (Wiliam & Thompson, 2007, p. 62). If teachers and students cannot use data tomorrow from an assessment administered today, then it is not formative. The most effective formative assessments give feedback immediately to impact learning at the point of need.

Research gathered in a variety of studies supports the positive effect of frequent assessments on student achievement as measured by standardized tests (Bloom, 1984; Black, 2003; Black & Wiliam, 1998; Meisels, Atkins-Burnett, Xue, Nicholson, Bickel, & Son, 2003; Rodriguez, 2004). The effect of formative assessment on student achievement has been documented as four to five times greater than the effect of reduced class size (Ehrenberg, Brewer, Gamoran, & Willms, 2001).

Another strong finding in the research on formative assessment is that the frequency of assessments matters. In the meta-analysis by Bangert-Drowns, Kulik, and Kulik (1991), percentile gain was measured over a fifteen-week course. The findings indicate that giving one assessment during the fifteen-week course resulted in a 13.5-percentile gain, while giving thirty per course (two assessments a week) yielded a 29-percentile gain in achievement. This is not to say that teachers need to administer two assessments per week. The greatest percentile gains were documented when five assessments were administered in a fifteen-week course.

Formative assessments also reinforce student effort and recognize progress toward meeting a standard. Students need to see the relationship between putting forth effort and making gains (Hattie, Biggs, & Purdie, 1996; Kumar, 1991; Schunk & Cox, 1986; Stipek & Weisz, 1981 [all cited in Marzano, 2007]). For real student involvement to occur, students need to embrace struggle as a necessary part of growth. This lesson is crucial not only for developing resiliency, but also for honing creativity, ingenuity, and entrepreneurship (Zmuda, 2008).

How students feel about tests and school plays a role in their performance; emotions can dictate students' response to assessment and affect their results (Stiggins et al., 2004). Students who typically do well on assessments will approach the task with confidence. Conversely, students who do not typically do well on assessments or don't feel confident in their understanding of the content will respond with fear and anxiety. Teachers have to help students understand that they are capable learners: "The power of formative assessment comes from the addition of student–to–teacher communication" (Brookhart, Moss, & Long, 2008, p. 53). Teachers must give students a variety of ways to demonstrate their learning. Frequent assessment *for* learning (formative) provides the greatest opportunity to build confidence and requires students to become partners in their own learning (Stiggins et al., 2004).

The Nintendo generation in today's classrooms is accustomed to ongoing formative assessment and minute-by-minute feedback. During play, student effort and progress are recognized. Students approach each task with confidence and enthusiasm as they strive to reach the next level in their games.

In the classroom, teachers help students understand formative assessment. Rather than calling the assessments *tests* or *quizzes*, teachers can call them less intimidating names such as "Show What You Know." Teachers explain that the students will be completing activities so that the teacher will know what they can do and how to help them master skills. These activities will also help the students know what they need to do to improve their work. In this approach, instead of feeling the pressure of assessment, students can work to do their best, and if they don't know how to do a task, they know that there will be an opportunity to learn without fear of failure or a poor grade. Students can show what they know and feel secure in knowing that they will have the opportunity to work toward improvement.

Student Guiding Question 1: Where Am I Going?

Students can hit any target that they can see and that holds still for them.

—Rick Stiggins

The first step in engaging students in assessment is to provide a clear and understandable vision of what students should know and be able to do as a result of a lesson, chapter, or unit of instruction. This vision should be stated in language students can easily understand and make their own. The second step is to provide models of strong and weak work so that students can determine the progress they are making toward the goal.

Students Articulate a Clear and Understandable Vision of the Learning Target

Education today is standards-driven. State and national assessments are designed to measure predetermined standards. Districts, schools, and teachers are utilizing a variety of methods and programs to meet the standards. Individual schools are translating standards and data from their assessments to meet the needs of students in their schools. In classrooms across North America, these standards are posted on bulletin boards, walls, hallways, and doors. Teachers labor to adapt standards into manageable instructional units. Given that state and national standards are written in varied formats and at different levels of specificity, teacher teams spend time making sense of the standards. They ask themselves two questions: (1) what does this standard mean? and (2) what would it look like if a student could do it? Teachers determine the knowledge, skills, and concepts students will need in order to meet the standards. These underlying knowledge, skills, and concepts constitute the building blocks for learning the standard and are typically called *learning targets*.

Teachers often use a process to determine the important learning targets for each standard. Teams of teachers unpack (Marzano & Haystead, 2008), unwrap (Ainsworth, 2003), or deconstruct (Stiggins et al., 2004) the standards to determine the targets. The students also need a clear understanding of the targets so that they can answer the question: where am I going?

"I Can" Statements

In the classroom, teachers help students reach a clear understanding of the learning target. They do this by developing their own "I Can" statements that describe in student-friendly terms what they need to do to meet the standard (Stiggins et al., 2004).

A common standard in writing is *Students will write a paragraph.* This standard involves a multistep process. We can begin to deconstruct the standard to determine the learning targets. One of the embedded learning targets for paragraph writing is understanding what a topic sentence is. To make this target clear to students, we might give them a description of a topic sentence. Then, using information about topic sentences, students can write a student-friendly "I Can" statement: *I can write a topic sentence, which means the first sentence of my paragraph will let the reader know what I will be writing about in my paragraph.*

"I Can" statements are used at all grade levels and subject areas to help students build a clear and understandable vision of the learning target. These statements can be incorporated into individual student plans for learning. Table 10.2 is an example of such a plan for a middle school science unit. The "What It Means!" section contains the student-friendly explanation of the standard.

Table 10.2: Learning Plan for Middle School Science Unit

Standard	What It Means!	Mastered
Science 1.1 Simulate how atoms and molecules have kinetic energy exhibited by constant motion.	I can show how atoms and molecules have energy of motion because they always move.	No
Science 1.2 Describe the properties of reactants and products of chemical reactions observed in the lab.	I can tell about the properties of what I begin a chemical reaction with and the properties of what is created in chemical reactions.	Yes, September 10

Students Understand Examples and Models of Strong and Weak Work

> To improve, students must know what good work looks like, compare their work to that standard and understand how to close the gap.
>
> —Royce Sadler

For students to determine if they have reached a target, they must have a clear understanding of what is considered exemplary work. As James Popham (2008) notes, "Student ownership of learning requires that students understand the evidence used to signify whether learning is taking place" (p. 81). An excellent tool for describing and defining quality work is the rubric. Rubrics should convey to students what constitutes excellence and how to evaluate their own work.

In the classroom, teachers help students understand what quality work looks like. To help students understand the difference between good work and poor work, teachers need to expose students to both. Many teachers do not like to share poor examples, but it is important for students to understand why work does not meet the standard and how to improve the work. Using rubrics, students can judge work. Teachers should present work samples that represent *each* rating on a rubric. Students can give their reasons why they think the work is good or poor. They can then discuss how to improve a weak piece of work. Students can also use work samples to determine the criteria for exemplary work. Looking at work, students can identify the traits or characteristics necessary for it to be considered exemplary.

When choosing work for students to review, it is best to use anonymous pieces of student work. So that students don't feel uncomfortable, teachers can exchange work samples from their classes with other teachers. This makes the work samples truly anonymous as students rate and decide what needs improvement to meet the standard.

Student Guiding Question 2: Where Am I Now?

> *Clear, concise feedback matched to standards will promote student achievement.*
>
> —Ken O'Connor

Once students have a clear understanding of the learning targets and exemplary work, they are ready to determine where they are in the learning process. Providing students with descriptive feedback and then helping them self-assess and set goals are the next steps.

Students Use Descriptive Feedback

In order to know where they are in their progress toward a learning target, students require feedback that provides them with useful information. Traditionally, teachers have given feedback in the form of letter grades, percentages, check marks, stars, and cute stickers. This *evaluative* feedback typically does not provide students with information about what they did well or where they can improve. Paul Black and Dylan Wiliam (1998) cite benefits to replacing this evaluative (judgmental) feedback with specific, *descriptive,* and immediate feedback. When teachers substituted comments for grades, students engaged more productively in improving their work (Black, Harrison, Lee, Marshall, & Wiliam, 2002). Anne Davies (2000a) agrees that specific, descriptive feedback that focuses on success and points the way to improvement has a positive effect on the learner and the learning process. Students must be given the opportunity to apply the feedback by trying again (Black & Wiliam, 1998). Utilizing descriptive feedback, students revise, practice, and retry.

Useful feedback, says Thomas Guskey (2005), is both "diagnostic and prescriptive. It reinforces precisely what students were expected to learn, identifies what was learned well, and describes what needs to be learned better" (p. 6). Descriptive feedback is specific and relates directly to the learning. It is related to performance and makes comparisons to exemplars (Davies, 2000a). Descriptive feedback is most effective when it points out both the strengths in the work and the areas needing improvement. Pointing out only weaknesses may cause a learner to lose the motivation to continue.

According to Sadler (1989), feedback is essential for guiding students through next steps. To use feedback effectively to involve students in their learning, teachers need to provide information that indicates to the students where they are in the learning. Students need to know how their thinking or performance differs from the goal and how they can move forward to reach the goal.

In the classroom, teachers provide descriptive feedback. Providing descriptive feedback requires more time, but the result is improved student work. Students receiving descriptive rather than nondescriptive feedback have an understanding of what they did well and what they can do to improve their work. Table 10.3 (page 236) gives examples of both types of feedback and points out the shortcomings of the nondescriptive examples.

Table 10.3: Examples of Feedback

Descriptive Feedback	Nondescriptive Feedback
Your topic sentence tells the reader what you are writing about.	B+ (What did the student do well? How can the student improve?)
Your narrative is organized with a beginning, middle, and end.	Nice Job (What did the student do well? How can the student improve?)
Many of your sentences begin with the word *and*. Think about our lessons on combining sentences and sentence fluency. See if you can combine the sentences or use various words to begin the sentences.	Don't use *and* to begin sentences. (How will the student fix this?)

Students Self-Assess and Set Goals

When students are required to think about their own learning and articulate what they understand and what they still need to learn, achievement improves (Black & Wiliam, 1998; Sternberg, 1996).

Results from a large number of synthesis studies indicate that student goal setting also increases student achievement (Lipsey & Wilson, 1993; Walberg, 1999; Wise & Okey, 1983 [all cited in Marzano, 2007]). The effect size of these studies is reported in percentile point gains. These gains range from 16 to 41 percentile points in classes where goal setting was employed.

In his book *Teaching With the Brain in Mind,* Eric Jensen (2005) states that having time to process is essential for learning. Learners need time to pause and think about their learning. Self-assessment allows the students to become active in their learning and to take more responsibility for their learning (Black, Harrison, Lee, Marshall, & Wiliam, 2004).

Self-assessments provide students with information about the quality of their work. They see ways in which the processes and products of their work are improving and can set goals for future learning experiences. Any form of self-assessment should ask students to review their work to determine what they have learned and what areas of misunderstanding still exist. No matter what form of self-assessment you use, be sure to give enough time for students to evaluate their progress. Self-assessment is such an important part of learning that time must be set aside during the course of the busy day for the students to reflect on their work.

In order to set reasonable and attainable goals, students can self-assess using data from formative assessments. Typically, teachers are the only users of assessment data. But assessment is not formative unless students are also users of the data. Stiggins (2008, p. 6) stresses that "what the students think about and do with assessment results is every bit as important as what the adults think about and do with those results." The most effective way for students to examine the results of an assessment is to go through them *target by target* and reflect on whether the errors were just simple mistakes or whether the targets need further study. It is important to teach students what actually constitutes a simple mistake so that they do not gloss over important targets.

In the classroom, teachers provide opportunities for self-assessment and goal setting. Student self-assessment can be complex or simple and can take many forms, including discussion (whole class or small group), reflection logs, weekly or daily self-evaluations, self-assessment checklists and inventories, teacher-student interviews, and conversations with peers.

A good time for self-assessment is prior to beginning a new unit of study. In *The Art and Science of Teaching*, Robert Marzano (2007, p. 39) states: "It has been reported that asking students to identify and record their areas of confusion not only enhances their learning but also provides the teacher with valuable diagnostic information" (Butler & Winne, 1995; Cross, 1998). Students can set goals for learning and create learning plans; teachers can use the information to differentiate instruction or form learning groups.

Before beginning a new unit in social studies, for example, a middle school teacher may give students a pretest and ask the students to self-assess their knowledge of the topic. On the pretest, students rate questions in three ways: (1) I know this, (2) I think I know this, or (3) I have no idea.

Students in primary grades can also rate their understanding of skills prior to the start of a new unit. Using traffic light icons (Black et al., 2004), students label their work *green* ("I know this" or "I can go"), *yellow* ("I think I know this" or "I can do this if I slow down"), or *red* ("I don't think I know this or how to do this" or "I need to stop"). Most importantly, the students know where they will need to work to improve their learning.

Once a unit is under way, students can use a rating scale, such as the one shown in table 10.4, to self-assess their level of proficiency on target skills.

Table 10.4: Geometry Targets Self-Assessment

	Measure angles.	Draw angles with a protractor.	Draw shapes using a compass.
I'VE GOT IT I can do this without help, and I can help others.			
I'M GETTING IT I'm beginning to understand, and I can do it with a little help from my teacher or friends.			
I'M STUCK I don't get it.			

Students can then use the information gathered from their self-assessment to develop learning goals. Goals can be written using a picture chart, graphic organizer (fig. 10.1), or form and then stored in a portfolio and checked periodically by the student.

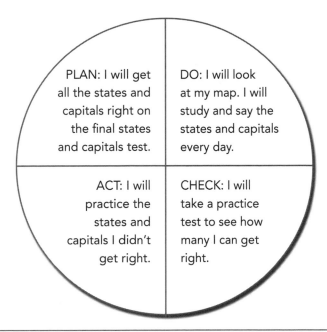

Figure 10.1: Sample goal-setting organizer for Plan-Do-Check-Act.

Student Guiding Question 3: How Can I Close the Gap?

I have learned not to underestimate the hand that students play in their own learning. . . . If students are taught the importance of using specific strategies, and what they need to work on, they will be empowered to improve.

—Susan Brookhart, Connie Moss, and Beverly Long

Now that the students have been helped to understand the learning targets, to determine what they still need to do to reach proficiency, and to set specific learning goals, the final step is to give them the means to reach their goals. Two strategies are particularly effective at this point in the process: letting students help one another with their learning and having students track and report on their own progress.

Students Support One Another in Addressing Gaps in Their Learning

Collaboration is a very powerful way to engage students in the learning process. In many classrooms, students remain an untapped resource. In order to increase student ownership of learning, provide students with opportunities to work collaboratively on meaningful tasks.

In the classroom, teachers guide students as they support one another in closing the gaps. When students experience difficulty, they can turn to classmates for support. Teachers in a middle school in Louisiana have established a system to ensure that students help one another. They administer frequent common formative assessments—short, with one or two specific targets—to determine who needs more time and/or support to be successful. Student assessments are checked and returned with only incorrect answers indicated. The students' first step is to refer to the textbook, notes, homework, and any previous assignments to try to determine why the answers were wrong. In addition, the students work in four-person collaborative teams. The team members help one another figure out what errors they made. After the students have spent the needed time to learn from their mistakes, another short assessment is administered to those students who did not meet the cut score the first time. For those students who still need more time and support, the teachers do small-group reteaching and then administer a third short assessment. If further instruction is needed, the teacher provides one-on-one tutoring before administering a fourth short assessment.

What is truly remarkable in these classrooms is that small-group reteaching and one-on-one tutoring are not usually needed because the students are so successful at helping one another. For students, it is a matter of pride when the person they helped passes the assessment. Their motivation to learn is evident as they work through the problems and ask when they can take the next assessment.

A first-grade teacher in another school develops a classroom system of support every fall. She asks students to make business cards that say *I am expert at* . . . The cards list things such as spelling, good ideas, math facts, capital letters, and so on. Every student is an expert at something. The teacher displays these cards on a bulletin board. The students must first ask an expert before they ask the teacher for help. These first-graders are motivated and want to help their classmates.

When students clearly understand the target and the difference between strong and weak work, they can also support their classmates by evaluating and editing one another's work. The most important part of peer editing and evaluating is to insist that students give descriptive feedback. It is not enough for a student to say he or she liked a piece of writing. Students must articulate *what* was good or needs improvement and why. Suggestions on how to improve should be a part of the editing process. Peer editors need to answer the question, What would make this work better? The criteria and rubric for peer evaluation must be clear and written in student-friendly language. Peer evaluators have the responsibility of judging the work against a standard, giving descriptive feedback, and offering suggestions for improvement.

Students Track and Communicate Their Learning

Tracking their progress and achievement allows students to be involved in communication and decision-making about the steps needed to close learning gaps. In most instances, teachers track student learning using a scale or rubric and a gradebook. Teachers could easily track the learning progression of the entire class using dots or bar graphs and then ask the students to track their own progress. In this way, students would be able to monitor and keep track of knowledge gained. This is very motivating and helps students target specific areas of need. Students should be expected to keep track of their materials and assessment information as well as their areas of improvement. When you ask a student what he knows and can do, he typically says "math" or "reading," not anything specific. If we ask, "What does this test tell you about what you know about fractions?" the usual response is, "That I know math." But when students track their learning target by target, they can actually articulate what they know and still need to learn.

In the classroom, teachers assist students in tracking their progress. Many schools have a standard related to the knowledge of content-area facts. Students are often given mastery quizzes. They can set a goal and create a plan for meeting their goal. Then students can track their progress by graphing their scores and asking themselves, "Are my scores increasing? Did I beat my last score?" This type of tracking allows the student to compete against him- or herself and minimizes the pressure of class competition.

Another way of helping students track their progress is to have them look back at previous work. Usually students are amused to see what their work looked like a few months before. Do they see an improvement? Has their work slightly improved, or has there been substantial improvement? If the improvement is slight, what can be done to gain more growth?

The culmination of student involvement in the assessment process is the student's ability to articulate and have meaningful dialogue about his or her learning. When students monitor and track their progress, discussions of their learning become more specific, meaningful, and targeted. Students have a sense of control and confidence. An excellent example of this level of communication is the student-led conference. There are many benefits of student-led conferences: (1) students are held personally accountable for their learning, which results in a greater sense of responsibility and pride of accomplishment; (2) the entire process is motivational and creates a shared responsibility for learning among the student, teacher, and parent; (3) students collect work samples that demonstrate their learning on each target (Stiggins et al., 2004). This evidence of student learning is usually saved in a portfolio that becomes the focus of the student-led conference.

In the classroom, teachers assist students as they communicate their learning. There are three types of student-led conferences: showcase conferences, two-way conferences, and three-way conferences. The *showcase* conference offers an opportunity for students to display their successes thus far; all the revealed work demonstrates growth and progress toward meeting the standards for that grade level or course. Students usually have an additional "work in progress" folder, but since this is a time for celebration, the works in progress are not a part of the conference.

The *two-way* conference is conducted in a group setting. Students meet with their parents at a designated time to discuss their progress thus far. Many conferences are scheduled simultaneously, and the teacher acts as a coach rather than a participant.

The *three-way* conference involves the student, parent, and teacher. In this conference, each participant plays a role. The student is expected to collect evidence of learning, reflect on his or her strengths and needs, and determine goals based on this analysis. To prepare for the meeting, students develop the agenda and role-play the conference with a peer.

The parent's responsibility is to gain a deeper understanding of the student's progress by asking clarifying questions during the conference. This allows parents to refine student's work by talking about school more specifically at home. Parents need to understand clearly their student's strengths, needs, and goals so that they can be more active participants in student learning.

The teacher's responsibility in the three-way conference is to facilitate the process and provide leadership for the evidence of student learning. It is also important for the teacher to reiterate the student's strengths, needs, and goals.

After a three-way conference, the teacher should follow up with each participant. Questions for the student include: "What went well?" "What would you change?" "Do you have a clear direction for your work?" Parent questions include: "What did you like?" "What would you change?" "Do you have a good understanding about your student's progress?" Questions teachers ask themselves include: "What are the successes?" "What areas are in need of adjustment for the next conference?" "What follow-up is required for parents who were unable to attend?"

We believe student-led conferences are powerful tools to hold students personally accountable, to increase their feelings of responsibility for their learning, and to keep them engaged in their learning. They also provide an opportunity for celebration. Hebert (1998, p. 585) notes that "learning is worth celebrating and children can be competent participants in that celebration."

Partners in Learning

The members of the Nintendo generation are poised to become partners in their learning if given the opportunity. This requires that we release some of the responsibility for learning to students by clarifying learning targets, providing descriptive feedback, guiding students as they self-assess and set goals, allowing students to support one another in closing learning gaps, having students track their progress, and facilitating student-led conferences. When students engage in their learning and take ownership of the process, they are able to set goals, evaluate their progress, and determine what course of action to take to reach the highest level of achievement. They become motivated, confident partners in their learning.

Teachers must ask themselves, How can we use the assessment process to help our students want to learn? Perhaps an even better question is, When was the last time we gave an assessment our students did not want to miss?

References and Resources

Ainsworth, L. (2003). *"Unwrapping" the standards: A simple process to make standards manageable.* Thousand Oaks, CA: Corwin.

Ainsworth, L. (2007). Common formative assessments: The centerpiece of an integrated standards-based assessment system. In D. Reeves (Ed.), *Ahead of the curve: The power of assessment to transform teaching and learning* (pp. 79–99). Bloomington, IN: Solution Tree.

Ainsworth, L., & Viegut, D. (2006). *Common formative assessments: How to connect standards-based instruction and assessment.* Thousand Oaks, CA: Corwin.

Arter, J. A., & Busick, K. U. (2001). *Practice with student-involved classroom assessment: A workbook and learning team guide.* Portland, OR: ETS Assessment Training Institute.

Bangert-Drowns, R. L., Kulik, J. A., & Kulik, C. C. (1991). Effects of classroom testing. *Journal of Educational Research, 85*(2), 89–99.

Black, P. (2003, April). *The nature and value of formative assessments for learning.* Paper presented at the annual meeting of the American Educational Research Association, Chicago., IL

Black, P., Harrison, C., Lee, C., Marshall, B., & Wiliam, D. (2002). *Working inside the black box: Assessment for learning in the classroom.* London: King's College.

Black, P., Harrison, C., Lee, C., Marshall, B., & Wiliam, D. (2004). Working inside the black box: Assessment for learning in the classroom. *Phi Delta Kappan, 86*(1), 9–19.

Black, P., & Wiliam, D. (1998). Inside the black box: Raising standards through classroom assessment. *Phi Delta Kappan, 80*(2), 139–148.

Bloom, B. (1984). The search for methods of group instruction as effective as one to one tutoring. *Educational Leadership, 41*(8), 4–17.

Brookhart, S., Moss, C., & Long, B. (2008). Formative assessment that empowers. *Educational Leadership, 66*(3), 52–57.

Chappuis, S., & Stiggins, R. J. (2002). Classroom assessment for learning. *Educational Leadership, 60*(1), 40–43.

Davies, A. (2000a). Feed back . . . feed forward: Using assessment to boost literacy learning. *Primary Leadership, 2*(3), 53–55.

Davies, A. (2000b). *Making classroom assessment work*. Merville, British Columbia, Canada: Connections Publishing.

DuFour, R., DuFour, R., & Eaker, R. (2008). *Revisiting professional learning communities at work: New insights for improving schools*. Bloomington, IN: Solution Tree.

Ehrenberg, R. E., Brewer, D. J., Gamoran, A., & Willms, J. D. (2001). Does class size matter? *Scientific American, 285*(5), 78–85.

Fisher, D., & Frey, N. (2007). *Checking for understanding: Formative assessment techniques for your classroom*. Alexandria, VA: Association for Supervision and Curriculum Development.

Guskey, T. R. (1996). *Communicating student learning* [ASCD Yearbook 1996]. Alexandria, VA: Association for Supervision and Curriculum Development.

Guskey, T. R. (2005, April). *Formative classroom assessment and Benjamin S. Bloom: Theory, research, and implications*. Paper presented at the annual meeting of the American Educational Research Association, Montreal, Quebec, Canada.

Guskey, T. R., & Bailey, J. M. (2001). *Developing grading and reporting systems for student learning*. Thousand Oaks, CA: Corwin.

Hebert, E. (1998). Lessons learned about student portfolios. *Phi Delta Kappan, 79*(8), 583–585.

Jensen, E. (2005). *Teaching with the brain in mind* (2nd ed.). Alexandria, VA: Association for Supervision and Curriculum Development.

Marzano, R. J. (2006). *Classroom assessment and grading that work*. Alexandria, VA: Association for Supervision and Curriculum Development.

Marzano, R. J. (2007). *The art and science of teaching*. Alexandria, VA: Association for Supervision and Curriculum Development.

Marzano, R. J., & Haystead, M. W. (2008). *Making standards useful in the classroom*. Alexandria, VA: Association for Supervision and Curriculum Development.

Meisels, S., Atkins-Burnett, S., Xue, Y., Nicholson, J., Bickel, D. D., & Son, S. H. (2003). Creating a system of accountability: The impact of instructional assessment on elementary children's achievement test scores. *Educational Policy Analysis Archives, 11*(9). Accessed at http://epaa.asu.edu/epaa/v11n9/ on November 3, 2008.

O'Connor, K. (2002). *How to grade for learning: Linking grades to standards*. Glenview, IL: Pearson.

O'Connor, K. (2007a). The last frontier: Tackling the grading dilemma. In D. Reeves (Ed.), *Ahead of the curve: The power of assessment to transform teaching and learning* (pp. 127–145). Bloomington, IN: Solution Tree.

O'Connor, K. (2007b). *A repair kit for grading: 15 fixes for broken grades*. Portland, OR: ETS Assessment Training Institute.

Popham, W. J. (2008). The assessment-savvy student. *Educational Leadership, 60*(1), 80–81.

Reeves, D. (Ed.). (2007). *Ahead of the curve: The power of assessment to transform teaching and learning*. Bloomington, IN: Solution Tree.

Rodriguez, M. C. (2004). The role of classroom assessment in student performance on TIMSS. *Applied Measurement in Education, 17*(1), 1–24.

Sadler, D. R. (1989). Formative assessment and the design of instructional systems. *Instructional Science, 18,* 119–144.

Sternberg, R. (1996). *Successful intelligence: How practical and creative intelligence determine success in life*. New York: Simon & Schuster.

Stiggins, R. J. (2005). *Student-involved assessment for learning* (4th ed.). Upper Saddle River, NJ: Merrill, Prentice Hall.

Stiggins, R. J. (2008, September). *Assessment for learning, the achievement gap, and truly effective schools*. Paper presented at the Educational Testing Service and College Board conference, Educational Testing in America: State Assessments, Achievement Gaps, National Policy and Innovations, Washington, DC.

Stiggins, R., Arter, J., Chappuis, J., & Chappuis, S. (2004). *Classroom assessment for student learning: Doing it right—Using it well*. Portland, OR: ETS Assessment Training Institute.

Wiliam, D. (2007). Changing classroom practice. *Educational Leadership, 65*(4), 36–42.

Wiliam, D., & Thompson, M. (2007). Integrating assessment with learning: What will it take to make it work? In C. A. Dwyer (Ed.), *The future of assessment: Shaping teaching and learning* (pp. 53–84). Mahwah, NJ: Lawrence Erlbaum Associates.

Zmuda, A. (2008). Springing into active learning. *Educational Leadership, 60*(1), 38–42.

TOM HIERCK

Tom Hierck is assistant superintendent of School District No. 46 (Sunshine Coast) in Gibsons, British Columbia. He has served with the Ministry of Education, where he worked with pilot districts on the development of a funding model that is school-based and connected to student success. He also served two years as president of the British Columbia Principals' and Vice-Principals' Association and was president-elect for the Canadian Association of Principals before assuming his current role. With twenty-six years of experience in public education, Tom has presented to schools and districts across North America on the importance of positive learning environments and the role of assessment to improve student learning. He was awarded the Queen's Golden Jubilee Medallion by the Premier and Lieutenant Governor of British Columbia in a ceremony at Government House for being a recognized leader in the field of public education. He is a contributor to *The Principal as Assessment Leader* (Solution Tree, 2009).

ELEVEN

Differentiated Pathways to Success

Tom Hierck

Don't tell me you believe "all kids can learn." Tell me what you're doing about the kids who aren't learning.

—Richard DuFour

All students have the capacity to be successful in school. As educators, it is our job to unlock the potential in all of our learners, particularly our most challenging ones, and point them in the direction most likely to produce the greatest chance for success. What qualifies as success will vary for individual students—education is a very personal journey—and will require from us a differentiated approach to instruction based on assessment data. In an era of accountability, data can give us a false sense of security. Data are important, but impersonal, standardized scores do not tell the whole story. As Carol Ann Tomlinson (2008) points out, "Few students will become dedicated learners because their standardized test scores increase" (p. 30). We have to create meaning from standardized test scores for our students. If we are to be effective advocates for kids, we also have to have other more personalized, individualized, meaningful data. When used well, data are evidence of progress. Taking the data collected and combining it with the other information we have about students allows us to structure a learning opportunity geared to success for all. Using data to differentiate instruction "calls for teachers to have clear learning goals that are rooted in content standards but crafted to ensure student engagement and understanding" (Tomlinson, 2008, p. 27). Schools should be about providing a sense of hope for all, not just achievement for the few.

As Thomas Guskey (2007) notes, "Assessments must become an integral part of the instructional process to help teachers improve their instruction or modify their approach to individual students" (p. 15). One of the anticipated outcomes of teachers adopting this practice is using what we learn from data to plan instruction and improve results for their classes. How and when educators intervene on behalf of students must be grounded in the data, and the interventions must be designed to meet them at their starting point and show them what they know and what they need to do next to carry their learning forward. We analyze the data from our assessments with that end in mind. As Tomlinson (2008) says, "Differentiation calls on teachers to vigilantly monitor student proximity to content goals throughout a learning cycle" (p. 27). This chapter will take the notion of an individualized approach a step further and suggest that every student *must* be successful if we are to move forward in the field of education.

Making Time for Individualization

Robert Marzano (2007) defines the three major roles of effective teachers as (1) making wise choices about the most effective instructional strategies to employ, (2) designing classroom curriculum to facilitate student learning, and (3) making effective use of classroom management techniques. Each of these components is critical to the creation of an effective classroom, but none in isolation will guarantee instructional effectiveness or student learning. The challenge of individualizing can seem overwhelming, given the range of students and abilities, not to mention our time constraints in delivering curricular content. A typical school year has perhaps 1,000 hours of instruction available—before we factor in disruptions. Marzano (2003) cites studies (Conant, 1973; Marzano & Riley, 1984; National Education

Commission on Time and Learning, 1994; Park, 1976) that suggest the *actual* total hours of instruction are closer to 696.

The solution to the seeming time crunch lies in the time we gain back when we spend less of it on behavior challenges and reteaching to the whole class. When we meet students' individual needs in a more systemic way, they engage with us, and behavior issues decrease. Research acknowledges that the number-one contributor to problem behavior at school is academic failure (Jimerson, Ferguson, Whipple, Anderson, & Dalton, 2002; McEvoy & Welker, 2000). We can't abdicate our responsibility to provide our best service to all students. The solution lies in looking at the individual and structuring the educational experience to maximize the strengths of that individual. Tim Lewis and George Sugai (1999) point out that "during teacher instruction, students go 'off-task' because (a) the instructional activities do not maintain student attention, (b) insufficient positive reinforcement is being provided, or (c) students access positive reinforcement from other activities or individuals" (p. 12). The teacher must make sure that all students are engaged at some level with the instruction and provide opportunities to demonstrate success. Karen Hume (2008) defines *differentiated instruction* as "effective instruction that is responsive to the diverse learning needs and preferences of individual learners" (p. 1). She goes on to describe this as a framework for all of the teaching and learning that occurs in classrooms. When we plan for this individualization before students are supposed to have learned something, we save time in reteaching after the end assessment.

Starting Out

So where do we begin? It seems appropriate that we look to the places and people most closely connected to the student: the classroom and the teacher. As teachers, we know that learning "takes place in the classrooms, as a result of the daily, minute-to-minute interactions that take place between teachers and students and the subjects they study" (Thompson & Wiliam, 2007, p. 1). What, then, can we do after the instructional phase when we have results that speak to varying degrees of student achievement? The important aspect of formative assessment is how teachers and students use the results.

Using assessment data to drive instruction helps educators answer one of the key questions posed by Richard DuFour, Rebecca DuFour, and Robert Eaker (2008, pp. 183–184): "How do we know when they have learned it?" Assessment and instruction are almost seamless in this ongoing exchange of information between teacher and student. Your role is to make frequent environmental scans to collect formal evidence such as assignments, exams, or homework, and informal evidence, such as the questions students may ask, their comments during group work, or even their confused expressions. The analysis of this evidence informs your practice and provides critical information as to next steps: "in this approach, assessment is no longer understood to be a thing or an event (such as a test or a quiz); rather, it becomes an ongoing, cyclical process that is woven into the minute-to-minute and day-by-day life of the classroom" (Thompson & Wiliam, 2007, p. 5). Guskey (2007, p. 15) suggests that if assessments are going to be used in this formative fashion and drive the instructional approach, teachers need to change their approach in three critical ways:

> They must 1) use assessments as sources of information for both students and teachers, 2) follow assessments with high-quality corrective instruction, and 3) give students second chances to demonstrate success.

Let's examine each of these in detail.

Assessments as Sources of Information

In order to use assessments as sources of information for both you and your students, you must ensure that you have developed appropriate tools. Rick Stiggins, Judith Arter, Jan Chappuis, and Steve Chappuis (2004) propose five keys to help guide our development of quality assessment practices in the classroom. Additionally, they propose some critical questions that help to clarify why each of the keys is important:

Key 1   Clear Purpose—What is the purpose of the assessment and who will benefit from the results?

Key 2   Clear Targets—What is it that we are assessing and what are the learning targets?

Key 3   Good Design—How are we assessing and what is the proper method to assess the learning targets identified in Key 2?

Key 4   Sound Communication—How are we communicating about the assessment and how will we manage the information?

Key 5   Student Involvement—How do we involve students in the assessment process and create opportunities for students to understand the learning targets? How can students monitor their progress throughout their learning? (pp. 14–17)

After developing and administering quality assessments, analysis of the results is critical. "Analysis" may be as simple as using a tally sheet to indicate how many students got a particular question wrong or as complex as a study of which students scored a 2 or 3 on a writing sample rubric. These data could lead us to analyze the question or assignment as to its validity. They may also lead us to look at our instructional process, as this might be the source of student error. If a majority of students make the same mistake, it's possible that the teaching, and not the learning, needs to change. Hume (2008) pushes the notion of analysis a little further by suggesting we speak of *evidence base* rather than *assessment* as this "emphasizes the wide variety of evidence that a differentiating teacher takes into account, including self-evaluations, teacher reflections, and an ever-increasing knowledge of individual students, along with the traditional range of formal and informal assessments" (p. 6).

Corrective Instruction

Following assessment with high-quality instruction flows naturally from this process of analysis. If we have identified learning difficulties, then we must take corrective steps. As Guskey (2007, p. 21) states, "If assessments provide vital information for both students and teachers, then it makes sense that they do not mark the end of learning." This is not to suggest that everything must be retaught every time. However, all students must complete the essential learning outcomes or building blocks for future learning. Guskey (2008) suggests that corrective activities should "present the concepts differently, engage students differently in their learning, and provide students with successful learning experiences" (p. 30). These steps, taken post-assessment, have the potential to help all students learn well.

A proactive approach leads us to consider our instructional approach with an eye towards differentiation. This differentiated approach is predicated on *how* kids learn and not *what* they learn. Hume (2008, p. 6) describes this difference as "understanding that there are many ways to learn, recognizing that some students learn differently than others, and providing those students with opportunities to learn in ways that work best for them." Investing time at the earliest learning opportunity may appear to be a challenge, but we see the end result in subsequent units as students become familiar with the expectations and the steps they need to take to close the gap. As Tomlinson (2008, p. 30) points out, "Teachers in effectively differentiated classes help students participate in the formation of their own identity as learners."

Second Chances

If we expect the majority of our students to learn the essential learning outcomes of our courses, we will have to provide second chances to demonstrate success. A first step in this process could be asking the student to analyze her own assessment and differentiate between errors that are simple mistakes and those that require further study. Consider this story shared by an educator who is also the mother of a third-grade student:

> My daughter took a third-grade benchmark assessment. She received an 81 percent or a B. We went through the assessment item by item and made a sheet like Stiggins suggests so she could analyze her mistakes. When she went through it, it was obvious that she didn't understand estimation, but had a firm grip on all four other outcomes.
>
> In the past, every time I tried to ask Maya about a mistake, she would get really upset and say, "It doesn't matter." When we tried this analysis, she loved it. In fact, she couldn't wait to get to the part where she made a mistake so she could decide whether it was a simple mistake or it needed further study. She had no problem deciphering simple mistakes from [topics for] further study; the simple ones were things she knew how to do and the areas requiring more study were things she had no clue how to start—for example, estimation. I shared the sheet with her a few days later, and we chatted about what I did and how it worked really well.

(Visit **go.solution-tree.com/assessment** to download an example of the sheet Maya and her mother used.)

Mistakes can be powerful tools for learning, especially if you structure opportunities for students to negotiate their mistakes as an ongoing process and not view them as a detriment to future performance. As students work through analyzing their assessments, it becomes quite clear to them and their teacher which areas require further study and what plan needs to be enacted to ensure students master the essential learning outcomes. This plan might involve further study (self-directed, peer-directed, or teacher-directed), reteaching (if a number of students made the same mistakes), or recognition that simple mistakes occurred (computational errors, for example). After this type of analysis and goal setting, it is essential for students to receive a second chance to work on the area of focus. In this case, Maya needs highly focused corrective instruction on estimation and then a second chance to demonstrate her deeper understanding and to ensure that the corrective instruction was effective.

It would be impractical to expect you and your students to engage in this type of activity for every assessment. As with any new initiative, start with a manageable target (one assessment per reporting period, for example), and build on the success you see.

The notion of second chances for students will be a challenging topic in some schools. It boils down to what you determine is the purpose of a grade. Is it to penalize those who did not get it the first time, or is it a descriptor of how well a student learned? In describing this latter view of a grade, Guskey (2007, p. 25) says, "From an educational perspective based on what is most helpful to students, this is clearly a more sound, defendable, and equitable position."

Walk Before You Run

Using assessments as sources of information, providing high-quality corrective instruction, and giving students second chances may be new strategies for you. Examine your current practice, and then systematically add pieces to your approach. The benefit to your students will become evident in both tangible results and the intangibles that underpin those results. Peer and self-assessment have the powerful effect of increasing students' voice and motivation: "it is very difficult for students to achieve a learning goal unless they understand that goal and can assess what they need to do to reach it. So self-assessment is essential to learning" (Black, Harrison, Lee, Marshall, & Wiliam, 2003, pp. 49–50, as quoted by Fullan, 2005, p. 55). As your students (and you) become more fluent in the process and expectations, self-assessment and student/teacher review become part of the regular routine following the assessment. The numerical results are one aspect of the assessment, but the real evidence of student progress and achievement (and closing the gap in their learning) comes in the analysis of those results.

Another form of analysis of an assessment could involve a group of teachers examining results and discussing what they see. To give this practice a "trial run" with your team, create a data set from a common assessment given to multiple classes (visit **go.solution-tree.com/assessment** to download a sample data set). Each teacher takes one of the classes and individually analyzes the results in three target areas (such as computational fluency, problem solving, and collaboration). Following this, talk with your three colleagues, and plan the next instructional phase for your combined group of fictional students. What are the data telling you? What ideas do you have around further teaching or reteaching? Are there individual students who need some assistance? Does one of the three broad topics need further review?

As you engage in these conversations, take note of your actions and reactions. In essence, you are establishing a protocol for future data discussions. A protocol is a structure of agreed-upon guidelines for a conversation. Once this agreement is in place, you can move to an examination of your own, real data and plan your next steps in instruction and providing feedback.

Effective Feedback

If we are to use feedback for instructional purposes, it must provide our students with information that helps them to close the gap between what they know and what they need to know. They may close the gap through increased effort and motivation or through a number of different cognitive processes such as "restructuring understandings, confirming to students that they are correct or incorrect, indicating that more information is available or needed, pointing to directions students could pursue, and/or indicating alternative strategies to understand particular information" (Hattie & Timperley, 2007, p. 82). John Hattie and Helen Timperley have established the significance of effective feedback; the results of their meta-analyses of factors that improve student achievement reveal that feedback ranks in the "top 5–10 highest influences on achievement" and ahead of factors such as "acceleration, socioeconomic influences, homework, the use of calculators, reducing class size, and retention" (p. 83). It's clear that feedback is important and that the quality of that feedback is critical. Provide descriptive feedback that is easy to understand and outlines the next steps for students to take. There are multiple sources of descriptive feedback in addition to teacher feedback. Consider peer feedback, student-created rubrics, self-assessment, or anonymous work samples as rich sources of information to support learning. As you move to this level of using multiple sources of descriptive feedback, students also develop a sense of ownership that is motivating and engaging. They will be able to gauge their own learning and growth over time while assuming greater responsibility for the outcomes.

Hattie and Timperley (2007, p. 86) suggest that effective feedback must answer three major questions asked by a teacher and/or by a student:

1. Where am I going? (What are the goals related to the task?)

2. How am I going? (Am I making progress towards the goal?)

3. Where to next? (What information is available that leads to more learning?)

Once you have the answers to these questions (lesson by lesson, unit by unit), you have made the connection between assessment and instruction and can support learning with results.

Differentiated Responses to Data

Given the diversity in our schools, classrooms, students, and teachers, it is important to have a variety of strategies and flexibility within those strategies so that you can contextualize and differentiate your instruction. Siobhan Leahy, Christine Lyon, Marnie Thompson, and Dylan Wiliam (2005, p. 20) have identified five general strategies that are "equally powerful for teachers of all content areas and at all grade levels:"

1. Clarifying and sharing learning intentions and criteria for success. [Do your students understand what is required of them and is it in a student friendly language?]

2. Engineering effective classroom discussions, questions, and learning tasks. [Are your class discussions and/or questions designed to gather information you can use for further instruction or to simply regurgitate existing knowledge?]

3. Providing feedback that moves learners forward. [Does the feedback you provide cause thinking and connect to what the student needs to do to improve?]

4. Activating students as the owners of their own learning. [Have you created shared responsibility for learning?]

5. Activating students as instructional resources for one another. [Do you use peer assessment to focus on improvement?] (p. 20)

As has been evident throughout this chapter, you should use the information you gain through utilizing these strategies to inform and adapt your instruction to meet student needs. In a similar vein, sharing the successful outcomes of these strategies with your colleagues helps to create a learning community of professionals who use results to hone their craft.

Reaching Out to the Hard to Reach

What are you doing about the kids who aren't learning? In a time of "too much to do and not enough time to do it," we need to invest in strategies that have a high yield and add value. We are fortunate to have many qualified and passionate educators who

> have a great deal of the required knowledge and skills to understand and implement the assessment *for* learning strategies once they are exposed to these ideas, but they need sustained opportunities to consciously develop, practice, reflect upon and refine this skill-set so that it works within the context of their own classrooms. (Thompson & Wiliam, 2007, p. 13)

Ensuring that every student learns and grows in your classroom is a challenge you need to meet. Our perceptions of students contribute to their classroom experiences. Mary Ellen Vogt (2000) suggests that when teachers work with perceived high achievers, they "encourage student interaction and creative approaches to learning, have warm and personal relationships with students, and offer extensions to learning including independent learning," while when working with perceived low achievers, they "prepare structured lessons with few opportunities for creativity, emphasize discipline and spend little time on relationships, and cover less content and acknowledge students for trying hard, but not for the quality of their thinking" (cited by Hume, 2008, p. 24). Some meet the challenge easily during each unit or lesson. For others, the breakthrough may take time. For still others, the gains are more akin to that of the bamboo plant, which germinates slowly for a number of years before going through a short period of extremely rapid growth. Tomlinson (2008) offers a key consideration regardless of where each of our students starts when she says, "What we teach must engage learners or we've lost them before we've begun" (p. 27).

If you believe that every student has the capacity to be successful, and if you adhere to the notion that this must happen, are you taking the steps to make it occur? Through a differentiated and individualized approach, rich data conversations, and a commitment to using formative assessment to drive instruction, your students will make great gains. As Guskey (2008, p. 34) asserts, "Engaging students in diverse corrective activities or exciting and challenging enrichment activities, depending on their performance on well designed formative assessments, offers the practical means to do just that." This is the work that follows the work you do day by day in your classrooms. It is worth the effort and the time to ensure that every success story gets a chance to be told.

References

DuFour, R., DuFour, R., & Eaker, R. (2008). *Revisiting professional learning communities at work: New insights for improving schools.* Bloomington, IN: Solution Tree.

Fullan, M. (2005). *Leadership and sustainability: System thinkers in action.* Thousand Oaks, CA: Corwin.

Guskey, T. R. (2007). Using assessments to improve teaching and learning. In D. Reeves (Ed.), *Ahead of the curve: The power of assessment to transform teaching and learning* (pp. 14–29). Bloomington, IN: Solution Tree.

Guskey, T. R. (2008). The rest of the story. *Educational Leadership, 65*(4), 28–35.

Hattie, J., & Timperley, H. (2007). The power of feedback. *Review of Educational Research, 77*(1), 81–112.

Hume, K. (2008). *Start where they are: Differentiating for success with the young adolescent.* Toronto, Ontario: Pearson Education Canada.

Jimerson, S. R., Ferguson, P., Whipple, A. D., Anderson, G. E., & Dalton, M. J. (2002). Exploring the association between grade retention and dropout: A longitudinal study examining socio-emotional, behavioral, and achievement characteristics of retained students. *California School Psychologist, 7*, 51–62.

Leahy, S., Lyon, C., Thompson, M., & Wiliam, D. (2005). Classroom assessment minute by minute, day by day. *Educational Leadership, 63*(3), 18–24.

Lewis, T. J., & Sugai, G. (1999). Effective behavior support: A systems approach to proactive school-wide management. *Focus on Exceptional Children, 31*(6), 1–24.

Marzano, R. J. (2003). *What works in schools: Translating research into action.* Alexandria, VA: Association for Supervision and Curriculum Development.

Marzano, R. J. (2007). *The art and science of teaching: A comprehensive framework for effective instruction.* Alexandria, VA: Association for Supervision and Curriculum Development.

McEvoy, A., & Welker, R. (2000). Antisocial behavior, academic failure, and school climate: A critical review. *Journal of Emotional and Behavioral Disorders, 8*(3), 130–140.

Stiggins, R. J., Arter, J. A., Chappuis, J., & Chappuis, S. (2004). *Classroom assessment for student learning: Doing it right—Using it well.* Portland, OR: ETS Assessment Training Institute.

Thompson, M., & Wiliam, D. (2007). *Tight but loose: A conceptual framework for scaling up school reforms.* Paper presented at the annual meeting of the American Educational Research Association, Chicago, IL.

Tomlinson, C.A. (2008). The goals of differentiation. *Educational Leadership, 66*(3), 26–30.

Vogt, M. E. (2000). Content learning for students needing modifications: An issue of access. In M. McLaughlin & M.E. Vogt (Eds.), *Creativity and innovation in content area teaching* (pp. 329–352). Norwood, MA: Christopher-Gordon.

Index

The Collaborative Administrator
Austin Buffum, Cassandra Erkens, Charles Hinman, Susan Huff, Lillie G. Jessie, Terri L. Martin, Mike Mattos, Anthony Muhammad, Peter Noonan, Geri Parscale, Eric Twadell, Jay Westover, and Kenneth C. Williams
Foreword by Robert Eaker
Introduction by Richard DuFour
In a culture of shared leadership, the administrator's role is more important than ever. This book addresses your toughest challenges with practical strategies and inspiring insight. **BKF256**

The Collaborative Teacher
Cassandra Erkens, Chris Jakicic, Lillie G. Jessie, Dennis King, Sharon V. Kramer, Thomas W. Many, Mary Ann Ranells, Ainsley B. Rose, Susan K. Sparks, and Eric Twadell
Foreword by Rebecca DuFour
Introduction by Richard DuFour
Transform education from inside the classroom. This book delivers best practices of collaborative teacher leadership, supporting the strategies with research and real classroom stories. **BKF257**

Ahead of the Curve
Edited by Douglas Reeves
Leaders in education contribute their perspectives of effective assessment design and implementation, sending out a call for redirecting assessment to improve student achievement and inform instruction. **BKF232**

The Principal as Assessment Leader
Edited by Thomas R. Guskey
Expert practitioners address the role of school leaders to model and spark positive change and ignite a shift toward assessments that drive instruction. **BKF344**